The History and Philosophy of Kung Fu: An Introduction

Danil Mikhailov

Philosophers' Circle

First published in 2012 by

Philosophers' Circle.

Information on this title: www.philosopherscircle.com/kungfuphilosophy

ISBN 978-0-9574340-0-4

Cover design by Dalya Dahrouge.

Cover illustration by Jon Spencer.

Printed and bound by CPI Group (UK) Ltd, Croydon, CR0 4YY

This book is dedicated to my family

Table of Contents

A philosopher who is not taking part in discussions is like a boxer who never goes into the ring.

[Ludwig Wittgenstein][1]

Preface and Acknowledgements

This book started as a series of lectures on Chinese philosophy, history and culture given over the past eight years to keen martial arts students in the Fujian White Crane kung fu club in England.

Each time, at the end of the lecture, the same question would inevitably be asked: What book could I recommend that describes how Chinese culture and philosophy is connected to kung fu? Each time, with a sigh, I would have to say that there is no one book that does the job and I would then reel off a whole long list of sources students might want to look at for particular parts of that story.

Eventually, it became clear that this book was asking to be written and I cleared a few weeks of time during two trips in 2011 – to Andalusia in Spain and later in the year to Hong Kong – and set to it.

The book that you are holding in your hands is not a manual that can teach you kung fu patterns, or techniques of internal cultivation. For that, you need a good teacher and years of dedicated practice. There is no secret in kung fu that can be used as a shortcut to achieving mastery without practice.

This book is also not a history of individual styles, their techniques and famous practitioners, although some are mentioned along the way. Rather it seeks to tell the story of kung fu as a whole, kung fu as a very specific art form that combines martial practice and ancient exercises of internal cultivation. An art form which is an inseparable part of Chinese culture. It looks into the origins of kung fu, its development through Chinese history and pays particular attention to its philosophic aspect.

If you approach it with that expectation in mind, my hope is that you will not be disappointed.

Any author, indeed any creator of anything worthwhile, engages in a series of dialogues both with the great writers and thinkers of generations past and with the experts of their own time. I am no different and I owe a debt of gratitude to countless people whose ideas have influenced me in one way or another.

The first thanks is due to my teacher, Master Dennis Ngo, who started me on my way to learning kung fu all those years ago and inspired so much of what I have been able to achieve.

The second thanks is to Sharon Ngo, a senior instructor of Fujian White Crane kung fu, who has provided so much invaluable guidance to me over the years, including by being one of the first to read and comment on this book.

I have spent many a happy year following Dennis and Sharon on our research trips to every corner of China, collecting footage of rare patterns, conducting interviews with masters and writing it all up as articles for the online magazine *Wushu Scholar*.

I am also grateful to the rest of the Fujian White Crane club: to my fellow instructors for their help and advice, and to the students who attended my lectures and otherwise peppered me with questions for their curiosity and boundless enthusiasm. Without them this book could not have happened.

A few members of the club in particular have given their time and expertise in different periods in the production of this book: Dawn Laker for her brilliant editing and proof reading, Jon Spencer for his wonderful drawing for the front cover and Dalya Dahrouge for the front cover's overall design.

Thank you also to my teachers at the School of Oriental and African Studies and at Birkbeck College, both in London, for furnishing me with the knowledge and the skills to conduct the research that underpins this book. Two people in particular need to be mentioned here: Professor Timothy Barrett for his inspirational teaching of the History of Chinese Religion – his classes are still my favourite from the year I spent at SOAS in 2002 – and Dr Brian Black, who has become a good friend since I first took his classes in Indian Philosophy and Buddhism at Birkbeck, and who provided very useful comments on an early draft of this book.

Finally, a huge thank you to my family, to whom this book is dedicated. To my mother Elena, for her love and support; my father Sergey, who triggered my life-long interest in martial arts by teaching me karate when I was not much taller than his knee; my sister Anastasia, for the many happy years we have shared; and last but not least, to my beautiful, kind and understanding wife, Shu Yee, in whose tummy even as I write this my little daughter, Olive, is waiting to be born.

A Note on Transcription of Terms

There are two transcription methods commonly used in literature to render Chinese words in the Roman alphabet: Wade-Giles and Pinyin. This adds a complication when dealing with translated material and is something any book that covers Chinese culture and history needs to deal with.

Pinyin is now the officially accepted transcription method, so it is the method I use in this book, with the singular exception of "kung fu," which is the older Wade-Giles rendering of what in Pinyin is "gong fu." However, "kung fu" is such a well-known phrase in the English language that I decided that using the alternative will lose more than it gains. All other terms, however, are rendered in Pinyin unless they are in quotation from another source that uses Wade-Giles.

Chronology of Chinese Dynasties

Xia ca. 2070 – ca. 1600 BC

Shang 1600–1046 BC

Zhou 1045–256 BC

> Spring & Autumn 771–476 BC
> Warring States 475–221 BC

Qin 221–207 BC

Han 206 BC–AD 220

Three Kingdoms 220–280

Period of Disunion 265–589

Sui 581–618

Tang 618–907

Five Dynasties 907–960

Song 960–1279

> Northern Song 960–1126
> Southern Song 1127–1279

Yuan 1279–1368

Ming 1368–1644

Qing 1644–1911

Introduction

Defining the Meaning of "Kung Fu"

Preamble

Imagine yourself transported to a day thirteen hundred years ago in the gigantic city of Xi'an, the capital of Tang Dynasty China. You are at the heart of the Middle Kingdom, the centre of the world.

A man walks home unsteadily in the dead of night. He wears no body armour, only the robes and girdle of a well-to-do gentleman. There are no bodyguards with him, only his old sword hanging from his waist.

A group of street robbers come out of the shadows and surround him on all sides, their broadswords and crude cudgels at the ready. The man stops in the middle of their circle. He steadies himself, his hand on the hilt of his sword. He is inebriated and appears to be an easy target. But as the first robber lunges, the man takes a small half-step to the side and twists his torso. His sword rustles out of its scabbard and in one smooth arc, nips the robber's neck. Blood spurts. The artery is cut. Meanwhile, the first robber long forgotten, the man goes low, to avoid a wild swing from another opponent, spins on the floor behind the attacker and with one clean cut severs the tendons just behind his knee. The second robber collapses to the ground, but the man is already up straight and his sword lashes out like the tongue of a viper, for the eyes, for the throat, down to the groin and thigh. Soon his opponents – the ones who are still alive – flee in all directions. The man wipes his blade clean on the clothes of one of his dead attackers, sheaths it and continues on his way.

Such a scene will be familiar to aficionados of Chinese martial arts films the world over, but what would you call the martial art that the mystery man deploys to such spectacular effect?

In the West and also likely in Hong Kong and many chiefly Cantonese-speaking Chinatowns around the world, the answer would be "kung fu."

In mainland China, however, the answer to the question of *what* the man was doing would most likely be "wushu", but if we turn the question to *how* he was doing it, then the answer will change to be about "kung fu."

To complicate things further (before we attempt to resolve them), consider another scene:

Across town at the same time, another man, no relation to the first, is engrossed in his work. In front of him on a broad lacquered desk is a piece of clean white paper, held down at its corners by weights of ingeniously carved jade. This paper was the great invention of the Chinese, the secrets of its making as yet unknown to the rest of the world.

The man holds a large horsehair brush perfectly perpendicular in his right hand, hovering just above the paper. The hairs of the brush are soaked in rich black ink the man ground himself a few minutes earlier. He calms his breathing, straightens his back. His left hand holds the sleeve of the right up and away from the paper. Then he presses the tip of the brush down to the paper, marking it with ink. Not breaking the flow of the line even once, his brush heads down, then up and across, then loops, then eases the pressure on the paper, then increases it. His wrist floats above the paper, the smallest movements translating into a pattern of dark lines on the white expanse below. One character appears, then two, three, four. The calligrapher lifts his brush and inspects his work with a critical eye.

Ask someone in China what art this second man is practising and the answer will of course be "calligraphy", but ask again *how* he is doing it and the answer will be exactly the same as with the first man: "kung fu".

This complex and unexpected use of the term "kung fu" in China is at the root of what this book is about because it begs two questions: first, what is kung fu? And second, is it the same as wushu?

Defining our Terms

In the West, the term "kung fu" has been used to describe the many hundreds of styles of Chinese martial arts ever since its popularisation by Bruce Lee in the 1960s.

However, when students start to practise a particular style, they quickly learn that each style has its own name, usually followed by the word quan, or "fist". So they practise Bai He Quan or Pigua Quan or Shaolin Quan, and use "kung fu" as just a collective name for all the different styles taken together.

In China, on the other hand, the collective term for all the different styles is "wushu", literally translated as "martial arts", and the term "kung fu" is used very differently.

In China, "kung fu" is used to denote the quality of inner strength that you achieve through years of foundation training and that gives the particular movements of your style their potency. Therefore your kung fu is dictated by the strength and flexibility of your joints, the speed of your muscles and, perhaps most importantly, the power of your qi, the Chinese term meaning both "energy" and "breath".

Tellingly, one of the worst insults to a wushu stylist in China would be to say that his kung fu was not good. It would be the equivalent of saying that he was all show and no substance.

That is why the swordsman in the first scene above can be said to practise wushu, but when we talk about how well he is able to employ his wushu skills, we talk about the quality of his foundation training and the power of his qi, so we talk about his kung fu.

As the second scene indicates, the term "kung fu" can also be used in China to describe a master's level of proficiency in art forms other than the martial arts.

It is still possible to come across people in China today saying that a calligrapher or a player of the Pipa has good kung fu, though increasingly only a scholar or an expert in the art would know to do so, as in everyday language the usage would be considered archaic.

When used that way, the term "kung fu" does not mean the master calligrapher or Pipa player also practises martial arts, but that the foundation training within their particular art has reached a certain level of potency or skill.

This makes sense when you consider that the literal meaning of "kung fu" in Chinese is quite simply: "hard work".

Looking beyond the literal meaning, we can say that the term describes the effort that goes into mastering any given skill and the changes in the practitioner's body, mind and spirit that take place through that effort.

It is these physical, mental and spiritual changes which allow the kung fu practitioner to move with the sublime level of skill visible to and appreciated by even uninitiated observers. And it does not matter what is involved in the movement, whether it is a sword, a fist, or a calligrapher's brush sliding on paper.

With this literal meaning of the words in mind, we can begin to define "kung fu" as *the achievement of physical, mental and spiritual self-transformation through the practice of a skill.*"

Nei Gong

The idea of self-transformation or self-perfection has a long history in Chinese culture and philosophy, as we will see. Particular practices, called nei gong, or internal cultivation, were popular among aristocrats as early as the Zhou Dynasty (1045–256 BC).

Nei gong covered a wide array of practices carried out at different times by different groups of people, but it most often comprised three key things: breathing exercises, meditation, and some sort of moving gymnastics, combined in different proportions depending on the particular school or classic that taught it.

All three things were explicable as working with different kinds of qi, as in the traditional Chinese world-view, every part of the human being is qi at different levels of its refinement or "density". So the bones, muscles and tendons used in gymnastics are a less refined and "denser" kind of qi, and the non-physical aspects such as the mind or heart (xing) and the spirit (shen) used in meditation are the more refined kinds of qi that connect the individual with the universal qi, or breath of the cosmos, and through it with the ultimate reality that is the Dao.

Nei gong was practised by some with the objective of changing your denser qi to qi of ever greater levels of refinement, by virtue of which the practitioner is somehow united with the Dao. While others, as we shall see, used nei gong like exercises for somewhat more mundane objectives of improving the health of their body, mind and spirit, and so achieving longevity.

These nei gong practices were a key method to achieving self-transformation for the ancient Chinese. So, when we talk about kung fu as "the achievement of self-transformation" in the context of a particular skill, like calligraphy, we are talking about the incorporation of nei gong-like practices into whatever skill or art form the practitioner pursues. Since the concepts of qi and Dao pervaded every corner of the Chinese world – as discussed in more detail in Chapter 9 – every skill or art form was seen as a process of utilising qi and following the Dao, and therefore susceptible to such cultivation.

Kung Fu versus Wushu

We can see then that the terms "kung fu" and "wushu" do not mean the same thing. Kung fu as a term is broader than the martial arts, though of all its usages by far the most common is the one associated with martial arts practice.

In the martial arts context, following our definition above, kung fu can be defined as "the achievement of physical, mental and spiritual self-transformation through the practice of wushu."

Since self-transformation in the Chinese sense was achieved through the method of internal cultivation of qi, i.e. nei gong, kung fu can further be understood as "the synthesis of nei gong practices and wushu" or, perhaps, "the incorporation of nei gong practices into wushu."

This idea of kung fu as the synthesis between older wushu practices and nei gong is the central proposition of this book and it is what I will attempt to present evidence for in the next few chapters.

It is, however, important to remember how wide the spectrum of qi cultivation could be, because when I talk about martial artists incorporating internal cultivation exercises into their martial practice, I do not mean that every single fighter cultivated his spirit to achieve a state of enlightenment or to become a Daoist immortal. Many would just have stayed at the lower end of the spectrum and focused on qi and breathing exercises and gymnastics to strengthen their joints and on meditation techniques to calm themselves before battle.

It is also important to note that it is qi cultivation that separates wushu from other non-Chinese martial arts, giving it its uniqueness. There are plenty of martial arts in the world that have punching and kicking, wrestling and weapons work, but only wushu and those Asian martial arts, such as karate, which were influenced by wushu, have such a well-developed theory of energy generation, breath control, meridians and pressure point striking, all of which are intimately tied to the rest of Chinese culture, religion, philosophy and traditional Chinese medicine.

This kung fu training with its focus on qi cultivation has become so integral to wushu that, today, every surviving style of traditional wushu incorporates some element of it.

This is why, in the martial arts context, it is quite acceptable to use the terms "wushu" and "kung fu" interchangeably. So in the end, Bruce Lee's use of the term to describe Chinese martial arts in general and its subsequent use in the West is not wrong. Kung fu is the essence of wushu – without it no style today can be described as a wushu style – so it is acceptable to call the practice by the name of what makes up its core.

In this book from now on we will therefore use the term "kung fu" in the sense of wushu which has its internal core of nei gong qi cultivation.

Only occasional references will be made to kung fu in the broader sense in which it can be applied to any art form, mostly reserved for the final chapter, "The Kung Fu Method".

Dating Kung Fu and Wushu

Although qi cultivation is ubiquitous now in wushu practice, this was not always the case. In fact, it is very clear that wushu, in its meaning of indigenous Chinese martial arts, is much older than kung fu.

The practice of wushu is as old as the practice of war in China and so as old as China itself. Rudimentary weapons such as arrows, spears and stone axes date back to the Stone Age. More organised warfare can arguably be dated back to the late Neolithic, 3500–2000 BC, on the basis of the archaeological record of indigenous weaponry and the beginnings of rudimentary fortification of settlements excavated during this period.[1]

Even if we attempted to limit the definition of "wushu" only to martial arts that were in some way unique to China, we would still be able to date it back with reasonable certainty at least as far back as the Shang Dynasty (1600–1046 BC), on the grounds that the archaeological record from that period shows the existence of particular types of weapons, such as the dagger axe ge[2], whose unique design would have differentiated Chinese martial arts from other ancient martial arts practised elsewhere in the world and yet still showed continuity with more recent weapons in the Chinese armoury.

The key question then arises of when was internal cultivation incorporated into this exiting wushu practice to turn wushu into kung fu?

The idea that internal cultivation is a key part of wushu is not new. As Peter Lorge points out in his excellent new survey of wushu history *Chinese Martial Arts: from Antiquity to the Twenty-First Century*, it has been a mainstay of martial arts discourse among educated literati writers in the nineteenth and twentieth centuries in China.[3]

In fact, Lorge makes clear that he is sceptical about the connection going any further back than the late Ming Dynasty (c. 1500–1600s) and believes any claims to an older lineage than that are a case of reading back into a more distant past something that is a relatively recent development in the history of wushu. He sets out the following challenge to supporters of an older connection between wushu and internal cultivation:

> "The historiographical question is whether the later system of practice [of Chinese martial arts] that relied upon ideas of the internal school and then connected up with medical gymnastics created a false lineage to legitimize itself, or whether it uncovered a progressive development of synthesized practice... The most reliable conclusion we can reach is that among the literate class, only in the late Ming Dynasty did serious attention begin to be focussed on martial artists and Daoist medical gymnastics together. Before that, any such practice was not mentioned, even if it did take place."[4]

Although Lorge only published his book in 2012, by which time I had almost completed my own manuscript, my strong support for the connection of wushu with internal cultivation has meant that my book can be read as something of a response to Lorge's challenge to find the evidence for a connection between wushu and internal cultivation prior to the Ming Dynasty.

In the process of looking for such evidence, I will show that one of the best-known theories about the creation of kung fu – that it was developed by the monks at the Shaolin Monastery as far back as the 6th century AD – cannot be substantiated.

But unlike Lorge, who reaches the same conclusion, I push the date of the creation of kung fu *back* to a thousand years before Bodhidharma came to Shaolin, rather than forward into the Ming Dynasty.

Internal Cultivation and the Army: a Contradiction?

Lorge's scepticism about the connection between internal cultivation and martial arts seems to stem from his belief that the military aspect of the martial arts has been undervalued in recent discourse because of the emphasis given to self-defence, health and self-cultivation. He states this quite clearly:

"Only by excluding soldiers and militiamen, who constitute the vast majority of martial artists in all time periods including the present, and focussing on the relatively tiny number of civilian martial artists can we make self-defense the main goal of martial arts training. An even smaller group of martial artists practiced martial arts, mostly archery in the Confucian tradition, primarily for self-cultivation."[5]

First of all, I agree with Lorge's observation that most wushu practitioners in China have been soldiers.

I also agree, that far too often, the core underlying violence of the martial arts is given too little attention. In fact, in Chapters 12 and 13, I will argue that it is the very violence inherent in kung fu that makes it such an effective method of self-cultivation.

However, I think there is no contradiction between the view that most who practised wushu over the centuries were soldiers who used it to kill, and the view that some small proportion of the wushu practitioners took their skill much further and combined it with the practice of nei gong to create kung fu. Similarly, there is no contradiction in saying that the function of writing is to communicate and that most wielders of the brush over the centuries have worked as simple scribes, and the fact that a few took their skills to new heights that turned their calligraphy from a functional skill into an art form, and again did so as a means to self-cultivation.

It is the small elite section of all practitioners, who can be called masters of their art form, who drive the art's development and growth. They do so against the background of the majority of practitioners who use their skills more functionally, as a means to an end, while they themselves make the practice the end in itself.

Lorge himself concludes in a number of places in his book that the skills of the rank-and-file soldier in the army were likely to be quite narrow. They would have been taught the use of a limited number of standard issue weapons, such as the spear or the broadsword, and even with these weapons their tactics would have been focused on working together in ranks to overwhelm the opponents, rather than showing individual prowess. However, alongside them would have been individual commanders and champions who had very different martial skills and a wider array of weapons.[6]

It is these individuals rather than rank-and-file fighters who, in my view, would have been most likely to have absorbed some sort of qi cultivation techniques, first developed as part of nei gong practice, into their martial arts.

It can be seen, therefore, that, unlike Lorge, I do not count just literati "civilians" when I talk about the elite practitioners of kung fu, but also generals, commanders and champions, i.e. all whose individual martial skill separated them from the rest.

It is also worth noting that during the Warring States to Han Dynasty period, where we will be focusing our attention in Part 1 of this book, all aristocrats would have practised martial arts, as Lorge himself points out, and, conversely, commanders and champions in armies would have overwhelmingly been aristocrats. Those aristocrats were also the stratum of society which was literate and which participated in refined practices such as nei gong.

Although not every aristocrat and not every army commander would have practised nei gong themselves, enough of them did that, over time, nei gong ideas and methods became an inseparable part of martial practice.

The trickle-down effect would even have transmitted some of these ideas down to the ranks, so simple soldiers may well have talked about their qi being deployed to help defeat an opponent, or using simple breathing exercises before battle, without knowing much about where the ideas first came from or ever practising nei gong themselves.

Overview

In Part 1 of this book, I will show that the kind of internal qi cultivation exercises that would later form the basis of Daoist gymnastics, could go all the way back to shamanic traditions in ancient Chinese prehistory. I will also develop the hypothesis that a kind of proto kung fu – an archaic form where *some* cultivation practices would already have been mixed with martial arts – is likely to have existed as early as the Shang and Zhou dynasties, though lack of written evidence from that time will mean that we will never be able to prove it.

I will then turn to the first period for which we do have such evidence: the Warring States period. I will demonstrate that internal cultivation exercises and longevity gymnastics first appear in the written record in such 4th century BC classics as the *Meng Zi*, the *Dao De Jing*, the *Zhuang Zi* and most importantly the little-known *Neiye*.

I will argue that, during the Warring States period, two sets of conditions for the creation of kung fu existed side by side: an indigenous method of fighting and range of uniquely Chinese fighting weapons that were passed down over at least the previous thousand years from the Shang Dynasty and, at the same time, the internal practices and philosophical mindset of nei gong that have remained a crucial part of kung fu to this day.

Then, looking at the early Han Dynasty, I will go one step further and show martial arts and internal cultivation exercises not only both being present but being practised together by the same group of people, as evidenced in the Daoist Classic the *Huai Nan Zi*.

On the basis of this, I will argue at the end of Part 1 that the 4th to 2nd centuries BC, covering the Warring States through to the early Han Dynasty, was the period when kung fu proper emerged out of the archaic and shamanistic proto kung fu.

In Part 2, I will sketch out how kung fu developed through later Chinese dynasties, reaching a peak during China's Golden Age during the Tang and Northern Song dynasties, flowering in the south of China during the Southern Song, Yuan and Ming dynasties, and finally entering its latest, modern phase under the pressure of the Manchu invasion during the Qing Dynasty.

In an attempt to put the developments in kung fu into context, I will start each chapter in both Part 1 and Part 2 with an overview of developments and changes in Chinese history and culture more broadly, before focusing on what such changes meant for the practice of kung fu itself.

In Part 3, I will go back and consider in much more detail the key philosophical principles of kung fu and how they relate to broader Chinese culture and the three great religions of Confucianism, Buddhism and, in particular, Daoism.

I will finish by delineating a number of features of what I call "the kung fu method": a way of living your life using the philosophy of kung fu that can be applied in any discipline or undertaking.

Part 1

Origins of Kung Fu in Ancient China

Chapter 1

The Early Dynasties

This chapter deals with China's prehistory and its first three dynasties. This was a time when indigenous Chinese martial arts and the internal cultivation practices that derived from shamanism were both being developed and began to be blended into an archaic form of proto kung fu.

China is the world's oldest living civilisation. Its written record of reigns and dynasties extends to the Xia Dynasty in the third millennium BC and archaeology points to continued settlement and cultivation of the Yellow River Plain for many thousands of years beforehand.[1]

Wushu practices, as we mentioned in the Introduction, developed early on in Chinese history and although they would not become kung fu until much later on, in the 4th to 2nd centuries BC, there were early developments in wushu which are crucial to the understanding of kung fu.

Likewise, there were early developments in philosophy and religious practices, particularly early Chinese shamanism, which can be seen to be precursors of the internal cultivation that would later be added to wushu to create kung fu.

To explore these early developments, we need to have an understanding of the historical events that shaped them, so it is worth spending some time looking at how the early Chinese civilisation was established.

The first three dynasties of China – the Xia, Shang and Zhou – were established by distinct tribes that made their homes along the course of the Yellow River. However, each dynasty absorbed the cultural achievements of the one they replaced, ensuring continuity through the transition and an intermingling that strengthened the Chinese civilisation.

A good description of this is given by Fairbank:

"...there seems to have been a rather smooth transition from the innumerable Neolithic villages of the Longshan culture to the Bronze Age capital cities of the Three Dynasties, all of which we can view as successive phases of a single cultural development... Xia, Shang, and Zhou centred in three different areas and seem to have coexisted... The Shang and Zhou "succession" consisted of becoming the dominant centre of ancient North China."[2]

Legendary Period

The Xia Dynasty, which began in about the year 2070 BC, is traditionally held to have been preceded by a legendary period of rule by the Three Sovereigns and the Five Emperors.

This was an age which predated the historic record and it is impossible to tell how many of these events had any basis in reality. What is certain is the importance of the colourful characters of the Three Sovereigns and Five Emperors in later Chinese culture. In art, literature, philosophy and even in politics these figures have loomed large, and as such they have become part of the symbolic heritage of kung fu as well.

The first of the Three Sovereigns was Fuxi, who is credited with inventing writing and fishing as well as teaching the Chinese about Yin and Yang and Ba Gua – the eight trigrams used in divination. It is believed that Fuxi ruled between 2953 and 2838 BC, or, according to other sources, between 2852 and 2738 BC.[3]

He was succeeded by Nuwa, who is remembered for saving mankind by repairing the damaged Heaven before it collapsed and crushed everything underneath it. Nuwa in turn was succeeded by Shennong, the inventor of agriculture. With Shennong, the era of the Three Sovereigns drew to a close and he was followed by the first of the Five Emperors, the celebrated Yellow Emperor, Huang Di (who is not to be confused with the much later, historical First Emperor of the Qin Dynasty, Qin Shi Huang Di).

The Yellow Emperor ruled between the years 2704 and 2595 BC, according to tradition, and was credited with creating traditional Chinese medicine and being one of the first great alchemists. According to Cooper, he learned magical skills from the Three Immortal Maids and from another Immortal on a mountain, "who, after considerable persuasion, instructed the Emperor in the understanding of the Tao, of sciences, meditation and medicines."[4]

Of all the legendary progenitors of China, he is by far the most venerated, being seen as the protector and teacher of mankind. All later emperors used him as a symbol of the perfect ruler and modelled themselves on his example.

In the 3rd and 2nd centuries BC, early Daoists would appropriate Huang Di as the patron and one of the founders of their religion alongside Lao Zi, establishing the Huang Lao Daoism (named after both of them) that was briefly influential at the court of early Han Dynasty emperors. *The Yellow Emperor Classic*, an early Chinese medical text, dates from about the same time.[5]

Huang Di was succeeded as Emperor by Zhuanxu, who unified the Chinese calendar, then Ku, who established the first schools, Yao, the inventor of the game of Weiqi (more famous in the West under its Japanese name Go) and finally by Shun.

Yao and Shun are the most venerated of the early rulers after Huang Di. Like him, both are seen as ideal rulers who served the people, upheld the Mandate of Heaven and, when their time came, both voluntarily gave up the throne to the person they judged to be the most worthy of becoming their successor: in Yao's case to Shun, in Shun's case to Yu the Great, the founder of the first historical dynasty, the Xia.

In addition to his role as founder of a dynasty, Yu is remembered as having been the greatest smith, architect and engineer, who spent thirteen years building a series of dykes and irrigation canals to divert the waters of the Yellow River, thereby not only protecting the land from apocalyptic floods but using the river to water the crops and increase the harvests.

Xia Dynasty

The Xia Dynasty that Yu founded in 2070 BC lasted for almost five hundred years. Until the second half of the 20th century, the Xia Dynasty was considered by many historians to be just as legendary in nature as the time of the Three Sovereigns and Five Emperors that preceded it. Part of the difficulty in looking that far back was that the Xia lacked the key invention of the Shang Dynasty that followed, namely a written script, therefore much of the information about its rulers and their deeds could only be found in much later sources.

However, archaeological discoveries of the so-called Erlitou culture made in Northern China in the 1950s, 60s and 70s, including excavation in 1959 of a site containing the remains of large palaces in Yanshi near Luoyang, started to support the Xia's historical existence, corroborating some of what was known from those sources.[6]

Based on this archaeological evidence, the Xia seem to have been a settled people, living in towns on the middle course of the Yellow River, who left behind a wealth of pottery, bronze implements and weapons and the stone foundations of their palaces and tombs.

The Emperors of the Xia set the pattern of future Chinese dynasties with a great and virtuous start, followed by a gradual decline and then, with the last few emperors lapsing into corruption and venality and so losing their mandate to rule, opening the door for the next dynasty to take over.

In the Chinese world-view, if the emperors failed to be virtuous and benevolent, then it was not only a right but a duty for another virtuous ruler to replace them. This legitimisation of the transfer of dynastic power would later be codified by philosophers of the Han Dynasty as the holding and the relinquishing of the Mandate of Heaven.

Shang Dynasty

The Xia Dynasty was succeeded by the Shang in 1600 BC after King Tang of the Shang Dynasty defeated the last king of the Xia at the Battle of Mingtiao. The Xia culture seems to have been absorbed to some extent by the succeeding dynasty, but according to tradition, rulers of the Qi state in the north and the Yue and Min Yue states in the south (in what are now Zhejiang and Fujian Provinces) draw their lineages from the remnants of the Xia Imperial House.

The Shang Dynasty left behind a wealth of bronze artefacts as well as tortoise shells and animal bones inscribed with the earliest examples of Chinese script. These inscriptions were used to divine the future and commune with the spirits of the ancestors. As such, these objects and the writing inscribed upon them were (and still are) seen as a link between the past, present and future for the Chinese people who crafted them and so as a way also to make sense of the world around them and their own place within it.

Since the Shang built their cities and palaces from wood and earth, little remains of what must have been impressive fortifications, so the bronzes as well as other archaeology such as pottery and tools, are the few ways we can get a sense of their civilisation.

This has meant that the cultural advances of the Shang are often underestimated by non-specialists: because there are no pyramids, ziggurats or temples left as a visible reminder, as is the case in Egypt, Babylon and Ancient Greece, the Shang civilisation is much less well known. However, one look at the intricacy and artistic value of the bronze artefacts they produced allows us to guess at the sophistication of the Shang society and the likely grandeur of their wooden cities.

Zhou Dynasty

Like the Xia before them, the later Shang kings grew increasingly cruel and corrupt. The last King, Zhou Xin and his wife, Lady Da Ji, were notoriously depraved, carrying out human sacrifices and once serving their rival, King Wen of Zhou, the body of his own murdered son to eat at a banquet.[7]

In the Chinese world-view, Zhou Xin's legitimacy was ebbing away because of his immorality and lack of benevolence, and his armies were finally defeated by Wu Wang and his sage counsellor and one of the first great military strategists, Jiang Ziya, at the Battle of Mu in 1046 BC.

The Battle of Mu holds pride of place as one of the most famous battles both in Chinese military history and Chinese mythology, because in parallel to the actual semi-historical battle fought by mortal men on the plains of the Yellow River, a battle of 10,000 spirits, gods and demigods was said to have been fought at the same time.

Echoing the Siege of Troy by the Greeks (which incidentally took place in 1194–1184 BC, just a hundred and fifty years before the Battle of Mu on the opposite side of the Eurasian landmass), gods and spirits of the traditional Chinese pantheon were said to have taken sides in the human conflict. Some spirits were believed to support Zhou Xin and others Wu Wang, and many of the mythological figures that were to endure through millennia of Chinese tradition to the present day first made their appearance or achieved prominence at that battle, such as, for example, Li Nezha, a popular war-like deity who wielded the famous Heaven and Earth bracelet as a weapon.[8]

After establishing the new Zhou Dynasty following his victory at Mu, King Wu of Zhou was said to have passed the reins of government to his brother, the Duke of Zhou, to rule as regent while Wu's son was still a minor.

Like Huang Di, Yao, Shun and Yu before him, the Duke of Zhou was revered by later generations as a paragon of princely virtue. He is cited repeatedly by Confucius as an ideal man and is said to have been, along with his father, King Wen, the first author of a commentary on the great Chinese divination classic, the *Yi Jing* (*I Ching* in Wade Giles) also known in the West as *The Book of Changes*. His commentary was so influential that it has been incorporated into the main text along with a later commentary traditionally ascribed to Confucius himself.[9]

As the Zhou Dynasty progressed, the power of its kings began to wane. However, the pattern established by the ending of the Xia and the Shang was now broken. Instead of immediately being replaced by another new dynasty, the Zhou persisted for centuries more, but in a diminished capacity. The power of other great aristocratic families controlling large feudal territories of their own increased until, by about the 8th century BC, the Zhou kings were fulfilling an almost exclusively ceremonial role as the head of state, while true power rested with the feudatories.

By the middle of the first millennium BC, Zhou China was, in effect, divided into a dozen independent dukedoms in cultural and military competition with each other.

The Rise of the Philosophers

This period in the twilight of the Zhou Dynasty, 770–475 BC, is known as the Spring and Autumn period. It is famous as the time when China's preeminent philosopher, Confucius (551–479 BC), was born, lived and taught, and when the Daoist sage Lao Zi (6th century BC?) was also supposedly alive. Confucius and Lao Zi are venerated to this day as the "founders" of two of China's great religions, Confucianism and Daoism respectively.

The use of quotation marks in the sentence above is due to the rather more nuanced and complicated facts of the matter now being uncovered by academics. First of all, it is generally agreed that Lao Zi's great work, the *Dao De Jing*, was probably written a good three hundred years after the time he was supposed to have lived. Angus Graham points to the 3rd century BC as the likely period of composition.[10]

The figure of Lao Zi himself may or may not have been based on a real historical person. As Lao Zi literally translates as "Old Master", all sorts of different historical and legendary figures may have been retrospectively combined under that single honorific to build the traditional image of Lao Zi we hold in our minds.

One theory revolves around Lao Tan, who was first mentioned in the Confucian *Analects* as the teacher of the rites to whom Confucius had paid respects. According to this theory, Lao Tan was adopted retrospectively by Daoists as the author of the anonymous *Dao De Jing* and the putative founder of their school, for the self-serving reason that Lao Tan's seniority over Confucius would suggest that the Daoist school was likewise senior to that of their Confucian rivals.[11]

Confucius, on the other hand, was a historical figure with verifiable dates of birth and death, but he was not a philosopher in the traditional sense of the word. He was not even a Confucian; or, at least, he would not have been seen as such by later generations of Confucians if he suddenly turned up and engaged them in conversation.

The historical Confucius was a teacher of rites and music, preoccupying himself with the correct performance of certain rituals in the state of Lu. He had students but did not actually leave any writings himself. Everything we think we know about what he said and thought comes down to us not even at second but more likely at third or fourth hand via students of the students of his students. The great Confucian classic, *The Analects*, which is said to record the Master's lessons, seems to have been written down by successive generations of his followers after Confucius had died and may not have reached its current form for over a century after his lifetime.[12]

Regardless of the historical accuracy of Confucius and Lao Zi, and what they actually taught, the Spring and Autumn period can be seen as the time when the art of philosophy was born in China, which mirrored a similar flowering of thought at roughly the same time in Greece and India, in what Karl Jaspers calls the Axial Age.

This begs the question of where these philosophical ideas, and particularly the ideas connected with practices of internal cultivation that we are most interested in, came from? What was the philosophical and spiritual culture from which Confucius and Lao Zi emerged?

Shamanism

The first three dynasties was the time state sponsored ancestor worship and divination activities were the dominant cultural activities in China, but it was also when shamanism was still widely practised among the population at large, and it is in shamanism, I would argue, that the earliest roots of internal cultivation practices lie.

The term "shamanism" is used to describe the religious and spiritual practices of a range of cultures spanning modern-day Tibet, Yunnan and the northern part of Indochina (particularly the homelands of the Hmong peoples), Mongolia, Siberia and both North and South America, although the heart of shamanism is generally agreed to be the land around Lake Baikal, the Siberian forests to the north of it and the Mongolian steppes to the south.[13]

Shamanism tends to be characterised by a holistic world-view that sees human beings as spiritually connected to the world around them, a world populated by animal and other natural spirits and the spirits of the ancestors. This connection allows mediums and shamans to use their powers to communicate with and control the spirits via trances, ecstatic signing, dancing and the use of hallucinogens. Two particularly important shamanic techniques are spirit possession, whereby a shaman's body is partially taken over by a spirit in order for the shaman to gain that spirit's knowledge or special powers, and spirit travel, when a shaman is able to leave his body and ascend into heaven or into the depths of the earth.[14]

The extent to which Chinese culture was influenced by early shamanism has been much debated by scholars of Chinese culture over the decades. Stutley, for example, believes that there is evidence for shamanic practices in Ancient China and that they influenced Daoism:

"According to the second-century Chinese dictionary, *Shuo-wen*, compiled by Xu Shen, 'the character *wu* [meaning shamaness] is a pictograph representing a woman who serves the "formless" and can by dancing cause the deities to descend'. *Wu* means both 'shamaness' and 'to dance'; male shamans are known as *hsi*... Shamanism entered China at an early age and deeply influenced Taoism (and to a lesser extent Confucianism) with its concept of an ideal society associated with matriarchal memories, the Taoist feminine symbol, magic and emphasis on sex techniques said to have an integral connection with the whole universe..."[15]

Stutley is not alone in making such claims. Scholars such as Chen Mengjia, Angus Graham, K.C. Chang, Julia Ching, Kristopher Schipper, Isabelle Robinet, Jordan Paper and Harold Roth[16] all support the idea of a shamanic genesis of the correlative, holistic characteristics of Chinese culture that found expression in later Daoism, and as such is of particular interest to our investigation of the origins of kung fu.

Angus Graham says the following, for example, of what he claims are Shamanic roots of the Warring States internal cultivation classic, the *Neiye*:

"...the meditation practiced privately and recommended to rulers as an arcanum of government [that is taught by the *Nei Yeh*] descends directly from the trance of the professional shaman... The shamanic origin of the exercise is plain... Its purpose is to clarify senses and heart to a luminous awareness, on the assumption which we are noticing everywhere in pre-Han thought that in the perfect awareness of the sage spontaneous motivation will coincide with the Way."[17]

Graham's observation of shamanic influences on the *Neiye* are noteworthy because we will be discussing the *Neiye* later on as one of the key pieces of evidence for internal cultivation practices, or nei gong, which would become a key component of kung fu.

On the opposite side of the debate are scholars such as David Keightley and Michael Puett, who opposed the theory of the shamanic origin of Chinese culture on the grounds that the earliest surviving texts and the earlier Shang Dynasty bronze and bone inscriptions do not provide sufficiently clear evidence of shamanic practices.[18]

The debate between the rival camps is technical and hinges on translations and interpretations of often fragmentary passages of written evidence and, where earlier periods are concerned, relying on archaeological evidence. For this reason, it may never be fully resolved.

I personally favour the shamanic origins theory for reasons that I present more fully in the end notes,[19] as they are not directly relevant to the topic at hand and perhaps one day would become a basis for a separate book. To me, shamanism is a clear candidate for the role of originating the internal cultivation practices that would later merge with wushu to create kung fu.

Martial Development

The time of the first three dynasties was the period when Chinese civilisation first developed its own indigenous weapons technology and fighting strategies, though fighting in the age of Shang and Zhou was very different to what we imagine when we think of kung fu today.

It was a time when the role of the warrior and that of the hunter were still very closely intertwined. Young noblemen vied with each other both in their martial prowess and their skill in hunting many of the exotic beasts that were still widespread across the Yellow River plains in those times, including elephants, rhinos, lions and tigers.

Perhaps because of its links with hunting, as well as its unmatched killing capacity, the most important and widely used weapon during the Shang and Zhou dynasties was the bow. In fact, Lorge points out that archery was the most widely practised martial art for most of Chinese history, all the way to the Qing Dynasty, when it was finally rendered ineffective by developments in firearms.[20]

The backbone of the armies was made up of chariots with deadly scythes carrying bow armed aristocrats.[21] Weapons of choice for infantry were the spear, the bow, and a uniquely Chinese weapon developed in the Shang Dynasty called the dagger-axe, or *ge*. Swords were only introduced into the arsenal in the Zhou period, becoming popular in the 6th century BC.[22]

In the Xia period, weapons were mostly made of wood, bamboo, bone and stone, but these natural materials were gradually replaced, first by bronze in the Shang period, and eventually by iron, which was transmitted from the southern barbarian states of Yue and Wu to the rest of China around 500 BC.[23]

Fighting during the early dynasties was ritualised and subject to strict codes of conduct:

"Wars were fought for prestige and honor more often than for territory, and combat was hedged about by ceremonial and ritual restrictions. Divination and sacrifices were performed before battle, and it was customary for the two sides to agree on the time and place before the action began. The *Zuo zhuan*, a narrative history dealing with this period but committed to writing several centuries later, contains many examples of restraint and what might be considered as chivalrous behavior on the part of the combatants. Commanders often refused to take unfair advantage of their opponents. In a famous case from 638 BC, the Duke of Song refused to attack an enemy force in the midst of a river crossing but waited until it had completed its deployment on the opposite bank, and in 554 BC an invading army withdrew from the state of Qi when it learned of the death of the Qi ruler. On the battlefield, warriors prized heroic feats and gallant gestures. Winning was by no means irrelevant, but the battle narratives of the *Zuo zhuan* often give the impression that the most important thing was to show off one's bravery and individual style."[24]

As far as open-hand fighting was concerned, there is only very limited written evidence surviving from the Shang and Zhou dynasties. In his analysis of early sources for martial arts, Lorge mentions some references to wrestling in the *Record of Ritual*, and references to early boxing called shoubo being demonstrated in public in the 7th century BC in the *Spring and Autumn Annals*, the *Guoling Commentary* and the *Zuozhuan*, works written during the Warring States, a few hundred years after the period they describe.[25] None of these, however, provide any detailed description of what was being practised.

Lack of contemporary sources means that much later texts, such as the histories and biographies of famous persons, which became popular from the Han Dynasty onwards, may well be our only way to try to speculate about what kind of open-hand martial arts were being practised during the Shang and the Zhou dynasties.

Salvatore Canzonieri mentions a number of early masters practising in the Spring and Autumn period, who he argues can be considered as doing "martial arts" rather than just fighting, most famously the Sword Master Yue Nu:

"By 496 BC, this was all to change, because of a great woman sword fighter, Yue Nu, who was considered the best in the land. She even taught the King of Yue's soldiers her sword fighting techniques. The Spring and Autumn Annals of Wu and Yue states that she was the first to develop the basic principles of sword and empty hand fighting as a holistic art form. She outlined the combination of position, breathing and consciousness, harmony of the internal and the external, offense and defense, and static and moving states necessary for developing fighting into an art form that was effective and efficient. By uniting these concepts, she was able to finally develop battlefield warfare tactics and fighting techniques into a martial art, rather than just military fighting."[26]

We must take such descriptions with a degree of caution because they are not based on primary contemporary sources but rather on descriptions of events written many centuries afterwards. *The Spring and Autumn Annals of Wu and Yue*, as the source used for the information in the quote above, was a 2nd century AD text and so written at least six hundred years after the period it is describing. As such, there is always a risk that the practices of the time *when* the source material was written were projected back into the time *about* which it is written.

Nonetheless, the description of masters such as Yue Nu beginning the process of going beyond the brute strength of archaic fighting towards ideas such as "breathing" and "harmony" in martial practice is not beyond the realms of possibility, as some evidence of a link between cultivation practices and martial arts does survive from this period.

The Development of Proto Kung Fu

During the Zhou Dynasty and the Warring States, archery transcended its direct martial function and became something of a symbol of the aristocratic and knightly (shi) classes. Because this was also the class which produced most of the great philosophers and authored most of the surviving classics, the potential for a link between martial arts, and archery in particular, and philosophical ideas and practices was already there.

Lorge points out that archery in this period had clear connections with ideas of self-cultivation:

> "...many thinkers used archery analogies to explain their larger points about morality. The audience for these thinkers was other members of the elite who were intimately familiar with archery. Archery became the first martial art directly connected to mental cultivation, that is, to a distinct mental focus transcending ordinary concerns."[27]

For Confucians, this self-cultivation was a way to demonstrate propriety, and archery contests became a ritual quite separate from its martial intent and even from any idea of competition. Confucius himself was said to have practised archery as a member of the knightly class, and he mentioned archery in *The Analects*, as did Mencius in his eponymous classic the *Meng Zi*.[28]

Later on, during the Han dynasty, we shall see Daoist writers develop this idea further and begin speaking of a more esoteric kind of internal cultivation, the objective of which would be not propriety or ritual but self-perfection and transcendence.

The dual link between archery and both war and hunting perhaps explains why archery became the first martial art for which there is evidence of cultivation practices, as it connected fighters in the Zhou Dynasties with far older practices in which shamanic and warrior/hunter rituals were linked.

If we take extant shamanic traditions in North America, Siberia and in corners of China where it is still practised – such as Inner Mongolia in the northwest and Yunnan in the southwest – as our example of what those archaic practices were like, then it seems likely that the spiritual dimension was part of the path of the warrior and the hunter from the earliest Stone Age times. Young men would have been initiated into the martial and hunting fraternity through spiritual ceremonies involving trances and spirit dancing, as well as separate but similar ceremonies performed before and after successful hunts and military ventures.

Interestingly, Lorge mentions that ritualised martial dances "that replicate movements used in combat, invoke otherworldly attention [from the ancestors] and assistance for combat, or attempt to induce a particular mental state useful in combat"[29] appeared in the written record in the Warring States period, though some of these records claimed "that they have reproduced or transmitted documents from earlier times."[30] How much earlier, of course, we have no way of knowing, but since dancing is a shamanic practice known to anthropologists from multiple cultures, it is possible to hypothesise that these Warring States performances merely continued a practice stretching back to prehistory, a practice where some melding between the martial and the spiritual worlds was already in evidence.

Lorge concludes:

"If by "spiritual" we mean connecting to some emotional, non-intellectual human need, or connected to the otherworldly spirits of the ancestors that Shang and Zhou aristocrats believed were present in their world, then these dances were indeed spiritual... More to the point, Chinese martial arts from the earliest times fulfilled a role beyond training for violence. This role existed before any of the Warring States schools of thought were formulated, and far in advance of the arrival of Buddhism in China..."[31]

We can argue then that ancient warrior/hunter activities like war dances and hunting ceremonies was the medium through which fighting and internal cultivation have always been linked, but it is only in the Zhou Dynasty period that such activities began to be captured in the written record.

These practices would not yet have met all the requirements to be considered fully kung fu. For one thing, the concepts of qi and the

Dao and the practice of internal cultivation that we have argued are integral to the practice being kung fu rather than just early wushu, would not yet have had the maturity given to them by the philosophical development of the Warring States period and the Han Dynasty. For another, the further back in history we go, the less distinct martial practices were from those carried out by other societies elsewhere in the world.

However, there are certainly enough of the elements in place, even if in a very early, vestigial form, that we could be justified in calling these martial practices an archaic progenitor of kung fu, a proto kung fu.

Chapter 2

The Warring States

This chapter covers a period of total war in ancient China, when martial skills and internal cultivation both reached their heights individually, but their blending into full kung fu had not yet been completed.

In the Warring States period (476–221 BC), the nature of warfare in China changed. From a continuous ebb and flow of competitive warfare between the states whose strengths were evenly balanced enough that complete victory or complete defeat were unlikely, it descended into total war.

The composition of armies also changed, extending conscription from only aristocrats and their retainers to include peasants as well, until almost all males of fighting age were drafted into enormous infantry armies,[1] armed with spears, halberds and crossbows. Such armies now counted men in their hundreds of thousands and not the tens of thousands which were the norm in the earlier Zhou period.[2]

With large numbers of men fighting on both sides, strategy and tactics became more important than individual martial skills. The role of the strategist and general eclipsed that of the heroic champion. Key Chinese military treatises such as *The Art of War* by Sun Wu (c. 544-c. 496 BC), who was better known as Sun Zi, or Master Sun, and a different text called *The Art of War* by Sun Bin (fl. Mid 4th century BC), were written during this period.

The separate statelets that the Zhou Empire had previously fragmented into eventually became seven kingdoms through a process of conquest and acquisition: Qin in the West, Han, Wei and Zhao in the central plains of the Yellow River, Qi in the east, Yan in the north, and Chu in the south.

These kingdoms were in an almost continuous state of war with each other over the ensuing two hundred and fifty years, until the balance of power suddenly shifted and one by one they succumbed to the state of Qin over a period of just ten years, starting with Han in 230 BC and finishing with Qi in 221 BC.

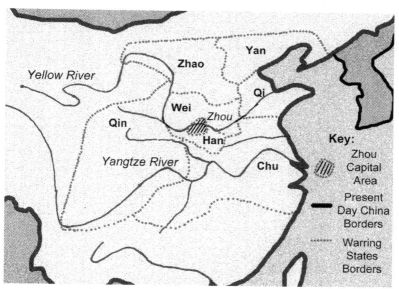

Map 1: Warring States

The Rise of Qin

Qin was able to triumph over the rest because of three key factors:

Firstly, being the most westerly of the seven kingdoms, it was more secluded and more protected by its geography – surrounded by mountains on three sides and bordered by the Yellow River on the fourth. In this way, it had secure flanks and was better able to choose the timing of its attacks on its neighbours, not fearing an attack from the rear while it was engaged in battle with another state. The more central states of the middle course of the Yellow River did not have such luxury.[3]

Secondly, in Qin Shi Huang Di (259–210 BC) it had a charismatic and ruthless leader to drive it towards its final ascendancy. Without doubt, it was the ferocity and prodigious skills of Qin Shi Huang that enabled him to achieve the kind of success that had eluded his predecessors.

Thirdly, the Qin government had leveraged the whole state towards its goal of military supremacy in a way that none of the other states was able to do. It was the famous Qin minister Lord Shang (390–338 BC) who started making changes towards this end. He increased the state's population by allowing land to be bought and sold for the first time, thus creating an influx of landless families from other states into Qin.[4] All males were then subject to universal conscription and "20 grades of military and civil nobility were introduced, based solely on the number of heads cut off in battle. The result was that everyone was not only willing, but eager, to fight."[5]

Such policies gave Qin armies their reputation among the other states for singular ruthlessness and barbarity. In one infamous incident in 260 BC, the Qin army massacred all the soldiers of the Chao army, who surrendered to them, in order to get their "quota of heads".[6]

Lord Shang's reforms were continued – despite the fact that he ended up losing his own head – by later ministers, who used the precepts of the Legalist philosophy developed by Han Fei Zi (ca. 280–233 BC) and Li Si (ca. 280–208 BC) to create a totalitarian state geared towards the single objective of domination over all others. Legalist philosophy demanded strict obedience of all subjects to the will of the king for the good of the state, judging all other considerations, including traditions, as being of secondary importance. In a time of war, this meant other considerations were not important at all, which allowed Qin Shi Huang to create the most effective military machine of his time.

The Hundred Schools

Alongside developments in the martial sphere, the Warring States period saw unparalleled growth of philosophical ideas in China, building on and reacting against Confucian thought and forming what is known as the Hundred Schools. During this period Confucians and Daoists developed their philosophies and competed against both each other and other rival schools, for example the Mohists, Yangists and Legalists.

The two greatest Confucians after Confucius himself, Meng Zi (372–289 BC) – better known as Mencius – and Xun Zi (ca. 312–230 BC), were historical figures with verifiable dates and writings. And although both were seen as clearly Confucian, they disagreed quite radically on their conceptions of the ideal "Confucian" society that should be built. At the root of it, Mencius believed that people were born good but later turned to evil actions, so the correct education and performance of rites should be designed to prevent that loss of original innocence, or at least to have people rediscover it. Xun Zi, on the other hand, thought the opposite: humans are born evil and selfish and it is through the benign influence of society and through discipline that they can be taught to be good, or else be punished for refusing to be so taught.

Mencius greatly influenced the Han Dynasty and the later neo-Confucians of the Southern Song Dynasty. Conversely, Xun Zi taught the Legalist Han Fei and through him influenced the Qin Dynasty and the First Emperor, Qin Shi Huang Di himself. So between them, Mencius and Xun Zi laid the foundation of the Chinese Empire, through the use of discipline and hard power to unify it (following Xun Zi) and then creating the bureaucracy, education and the cult of the benign emperor needed to govern it (following Mencius).

The second great Daoist philosopher after Lao Zi was Zhuang Zi (369–286 BC), a near contemporary of Mencius if we accept evidence for the dates of his birth and death given by the great Han Dynasty historian Sima Qian. There is little other evidence for Zhuang Zi's life, and although scholars such as Angus Graham believe Zhuang Zi to have been a real person, they have pointed out that some of the chapters of his eponymous classic work were likely written by other people at a later date and then compiled together with the original first seven chapters which were written by Zhuang Zi himself. More so than with Lao Zi's *Dao De Jing*, however, there is an internal consistency in tone of voice and coherency in message within at least these seven inner chapters of the *Zhuang Zi*. This humorous but profound voice connects the text to the popular image of Zhuang Zi, so in this case the book itself acts as evidence for what the historical Zhuang Zi was like.

Zhuang Zi's thinking is characterised by his scepticism towards set ideas and recognised authority, his irreverent humour and calm acceptance of the rhythms of life, including its inevitable ending in death. It is Zhuang Zi, as we shall discuss in much more detail in Part 3, who has left us the earliest description of the process of perfecting oneself that is at the core of kung fu practice.

The Chan (Zen) Buddhists looked back to Zhuang Zi as an early influence and have used his aphorisms and stories as the original prototype for the Zen Buddhist koan – the nonsensical statement that was used to trigger a deeper intuitive understanding in the interlocutor.

Daoism, Confucianism and Legalism, as well as other key schools, for example, the Yangists and the Mohists that we do not have space to discuss here, together offered an impressive array of rival ideas for how to organise the state, but many of their works have been lost to subsequent generations in the Great Burning of the Books ordered by Qin Shi Huang Di when he ascended the throne of a newly unified China as First Emperor.

Qin Shi Huang saw first hand how the power of just one school, the Legalists, made the crucial difference that allowed him to defeat his rivals. He was not about to allow other rival ideas, that could easily unseat him, to exist outside of his control.

Qin Shi Huang was a pivotal figure in China's history, and to counterbalance the destruction caused by his wars and the Great Burning, he also created much that would later form the backbone of Chinese civilisation. Not least among his acts was the institution of a single written script that for the first time allowed his subjects, many of whose languages were mutually incomprehensible, to understand each other directly. This in turn lay the foundation of a shared literature and a shared corpus of knowledge. Qin Shi Huang also ordered the standardisation of weights, measures and coinage across the Empire, improving trade, and ordered the Great Wall to be constructed to protect China from its restive barbarian neighbours in the steppes to the north and west.

In short, Qin Shi Huang fully justified his title of First Emperor by truly knitting together, for the first time, what used to be sometimes only a loosely connected patchwork of states and nations.

His achievements were made at great cost, however, and it is perhaps not surprising that shortly after his death, his heir, the teenage Second Emperor, was murdered and the Qin Dynasty was overthrown. Though the Qin Dynasty only lasted for just over twenty years, the structures it left behind and the very shape of Chinese Empire would last for over two millennia and are still recognisable today.

Martial Developments

The Warring States was a period when the two crucial ingredients that make kung fu – namely indigenous Chinese martial skills and internal cultivation practices – both reached a high point of development.

The shamanic internal cultivation practices of proto kung fu were now fully developed and widely practised, not only among groups who would later be called Daoists, but also among the so-called followers of Peng Zu (the ancient Chinese sage famed for his longevity) who focused on the physical rather than the spiritual benefits of exercises such as breath control and gymnastics to improve their health and attain longevity.[7]

The Daoist version of the cultivation practices was given a profound philosophical basis by figures such as Zhuang Zi and the anonymous writer of the *Dao De Jing* (who was not likely to have been Lao Zi himself, as we have already mentioned). However, the clearest and most comprehensive summary of such practices from the Warring States period can be found in the relatively little-known *Neiye* classic.

As we will discuss in the next chapter, the *Neiye* should rightly be seen as the key missing piece of the puzzle that links Daoism, and Chinese philosophy more broadly, with kung fu, through its emphasis on the use of the body, and not just the mind, in self-cultivation.

On the martial side of kung fu advancements, apart from the huge leap forward in military strategy, the Warring States period also saw a number of key developments in weapons that had an influence on future military and martial application, such as the creation of Chinese cavalry, including the introduction of cavalry archers from the nomadic Xiong Nu tribes by King Wuling of Zhao in 307 BC, the addition of crossbows and siege engines into the arsenal of war,[8] as well as the introduction of leather-plated and lacquered lamellar armour and the wide adaption of iron swords.[9]

Although on the surface, this period seems the perfect time for the creation of kung fu, it is worth noting that none of the key military classics of the period, such as the works of Sun Zi and Sun Bin, mention developments in individual martial skills and their combination with nei gong. Instead, they focused on strategy, generalship and all the necessary skills to command large armies of men.

Certainly there is no doubt that officers and generals would have possessed a high level of individual martial skill, and there is mention of "sword dances" and "shield dances" being performed at banquets to demonstrate skills in arms (in, for example, Qu Yuan's *Songs of the South*,[10] composed in the 4th century BC, and in accounts of the Emperor Gaozu of Han's rise to power in the 3rd century BC[11]), which could refer to what we would call patterns or taulu today. But such mentions of individual martial skill are very rare and peripheral compared to the emphasis given to strategy.

The fact that individual martial practices and nei gong are not specifically mentioned does not mean, of course, that they were not in existence at the time. It could mean quite the opposite: that they were so universally known and ingrained in martial practice that they did not require mention in the military classics.

There is also an argument to be made that, under conditions of mass warfare such as existed in the Warring States period, it was only natural that strategists rather than individual fighters attracted most mention in military classics.

It would make sense that, in an era of multiple kingdoms fighting against each other in large-scale battles with rank formation, that the strategic and tactical skills of a general would be seen as more important to his success than perhaps his own martial prowess. Also, for that matter, the ability of his troops to manoeuvre and act in concert might count for more than the sum total of their individual skills with weapons.

We have already seen that the term "kung fu" can cover many different forms of activity where effort is exerted in the perfection of a skill. The martial arts application is simply the most common and best-known usage of the term. So we must consider that this term can be equally well applied to the development and execution of a military strategy by a general, as taught by Sun Zi, as it can to the development of that general's own martial skill.

In other words, the art of the strategist *was* still kung fu, just a different kung fu, suited to its time and context.

I will return to this argument in more detail in Part 3, Chapter 12 and show there is some evidence that internal cultivation techniques may have been used by strategists in the way we have argued is required for martial practice to be seen to really be kung fu.

All in all, therefore, the Warring States period had the two key prerequisites for the existence of kung fu both at the apex of their development, but no direct and unambiguous written evidence yet of them being put together.

Chapter 3

The Missing Piece of the Puzzle

This chapter analyses a key text in the history of Daoism: the Neiye. *This text has some of the fullest and earliest recorded evidence for internal cultivation practice of nei gong, which would later be used in a whole range of related exercises, from qi gong and daoyin gymnastics to kung fu.*

Popular writers about Daoist philosophy far too often put a full stop after introducing Lao Zi and Zhuang Zi as the two great philosophers of Daoism, as if the rest of the two-and-a-half millennia of Daoist thought and practice had nothing of interest to offer.

That is partly to do with a lack of translated material of, for example, the hundreds of Daoist classics from the Period of Disunity and the Tang and Song Dynasties, a sad state of affairs which modern scholars have only recently begun to rectify.

However, it is also due to a kind of prejudice in academic philosophy circles against any theories that involve physical practice, which is too often viewed with suspicion by scholars or dismissed altogether as inherently inferior to "purer" philosophical ideas.

But it is the marrying together of physical practice and intellectual insight within Daoism, and within Chinese philosophy as a whole, which is of course of the greatest interest to anyone trying to understand the philosophy of kung fu, to which the combination of the mental and the physical is absolutely integral.

Undoubtedly the most important physical practice as far as kung fu is concerned is the internal cultivation called nei gong. The earliest mentions of such internal cultivation exercises in Daoist sources (we have already mentioned some earlier hints of internal cultivation, focused on the art of archery, that can be found in non-Daoist and particularly Confucian sources) occur in a number of Warring States period classics from the 4th and 3rd centuries BC, including the *Dao De Jing* and the *Zhuang Zi*, but certainly not limited to them.

Zhuang Zi, for example, mentioned that correct breathing was a mark of the Perfected Man. In fact, he left us with one of the most potent metaphors for breath practice that has been quoted by Daoists and qi gong Masters ever since:

"The True Men of old... breathed from their deepest depths... The breathing of the True Man is from down in his heels, the breathing of plain men is from their throats; as for the cowed, the submissive, they talk in gulps as though retching..."[1]

In another story, Zhuang Zi seems to be describing a sage entering into a state of meditation through the emptying of his heart/mind, xing:[2]

"Tzu-ch'i of Nan-kuo reclined elbow on armrest, looked up at the sky and exhaled, in a trance as though he had lost the counterpart of himself... 'This time I had lost my own self, did you know it?' [Tzuch'i said, after coming out of his trance]"[3]

Lao Zi, meanwhile, talked about both breathing and meditative practices, using a common metaphor of the mirror to represent the heart/mind of the practitioner:

"In concentrating your breath can you become as supple as a babe? Can you polish your mysterious mirror and leave no blemish?"[4]

Though, for the sake of balance, it should also be noted that in one passage he seems to be criticising excessive breath and energy practice:

"To know harmony is called the constant;
To know the constant is called discernment.
To try to add to one's vitality is called ill-omened;
For the mind to egg on the breath is called violent."[5]

This makes sense if we remember that Lao Zi held emptiness and inaction as the surest road to a unity with the Dao. In his eye anything pursued too actively and in excess, including, one must reason, nei gong practice, would take the ruler away from that road.

Aside from these tantalising references in the *Dao De Jing* and the *Zhuang Zi*, the first sustained and fully developed textual evidence for nei gong is found in the third great Daoist classic of the late Warring States: the *Neiye*, which has remained much less well known outside the academic community than its illustrious rivals.

Analysis of the *Neiye*

The *Neiye* is a short text dating from the mid-4th century BC. According to Roth, it was most likely composed by philosophers working in the great Qi Xia academy in the State of Qi and was included in the compendium of other works from the Qi Xia, called the *Guanzi*.[6]

The *Neiye*'s particular teachings were then popularised through their influence on the much better-known eclectic compendium of mostly Daoist knowledge produced at the court of Liu An, the Prince of Huai Nan, in the 2nd century BC, called the *Huai Nan Zi*.[7]

The *Neiye*, like the *Zhuang Zi* and the *Dao De Jing*, talks about self-cultivation, or becoming a Perfected Man (of which I will talk more in Chapter 10), but unlike the other two classics it does not shy away from the physical and practical aspects of doing so. Instead, it exalts them in a way no other classic of the period comes close to doing.

It deals with the health and wellbeing of the practitioner, achieved through correct breathing and correct posture:

"When your body is not aligned,
The inner power will not come.
When you are not tranquil within,
Your mind will not be well ordered.
Align your body, assist the inner power,
Then it will gradually come on its own."[8]
"... If people can be aligned and tranquil,
Their skin will be ample and smooth,
Their ears and eyes will be acute and clear,
Their muscles will be supple and their bones will be strong.
They will then be able to hold up the Great Circle [of the heavens]
And tread firmly over the Great Square [of the earth]."[9]

The *Neiye* distinguishes itself by not only mentioning the importance of posture and breathing, but by also describing the required movements of the body to a level of detail not found in other, more intellectualised classics:

"... For all [to practice] this Way:
You must coil, you must contract,
You must uncoil, you must expand,
You must be firm, you must be regular [in this practice].
Hold fast to this excellent [practice]; do not let go of it.
Chase away the excessive; abandon the trivial.
And when you reach its ultimate limit
You will return to the Way and its inner power."[10]

It clearly unites, for the first time, the three areas important to future nei gong (and later kung fu) practices: body, through its correct alignment; mind, through its focus and state of unity with the Way; and breath, through its concentration and refinement to produce a greater energy.

All three combine in a single approach to cultivation:

"... By concentrating your vital breath as if numinous,
The myriad things will all be contained within you.
Can you concentrate? Can you unite with them?
... When the four limbs are aligned
And the blood and vital breath are tranquil,
Unify your awareness, concentrate your mind,
Then your eyes and ears will not be overstimulated.
And even the far-off will seem close at hand."[11]

Harold Roth interprets the objective of the internal cultivation advocated in the *Neiye* as "attaining the numinous "mind within the mind", the nondual awareness of the Way".[12]

The key metaphysical insight is that each person is in a state of monistic unity with the Universe but we are not aware of this unity because of the constant distractions provided by our thoughts, emotions and perceptions. The three-part practice of correct alignment of the body, correct breathing and the stilling and emptying of the mind, allows us a moment of realisation or enlightenment when we experience this unity directly. Once that happens, our objective is then, through continuing practice, to attempt to retain that awareness.

Roth distinguishes between the introvertive mystical experience during that initial moment of awareness of unity with the Way achieved by the practitioner, and the subsequent extrovertive experience where the memory of the unity is retained even as the practitioner enters back into his everyday life, seeing both the "unity and the multiplicity" of things.[13]

Roth is quite clear that physical alignment of the body is one of the key aspects of such cultivation, placing it as part of a "Fourfold Aligning" of, firstly, the body, then the four limbs, then the vital energy or breath, qi, and finally the mind.[14] However, he reads the *Neiye* passages concerning the alignment of the body and the limbs as describing only the traditional sitting meditation position practised across Asia.[15]

Perhaps because of my own practice, I read the descriptions of physical alignment differently from Roth. Yes, the mentions of straightness, stability and squareness could refer to a sitting posture as Roth assumes, but they could just as easily refer to a variety of standing postures which are common in styles of qi gong surviving to this day.

Other mentions of, for example, "coiling" and "uncoiling" could just refer to the internal movements of the abdomen and the diaphragm during breathing, but could also indicate movement within postures or between postures. And lines such as "If when full you don't move quickly, vital energy will not circulate to your limbs"[16] are even clearer as evidence of movement.

The *Neiye* is not specific enough for us to be sure exactly which movements are discussed, but it is clear that movement of some sort, rather than or as well as static meditation, was involved. This of course is an important link with modern-day qi gong exercises, where both movement and stillness are involved, and, by extension, with kung fu.

Extending his analysis to include Daoism more generally, Roth argues that the *Neiye* is crucial for the understanding of early Daoism, being the earliest text that gives cultivation practices its central focus, rather than, like the *Dao De Jing* and *Zhuang Zi*, just mentioning them in passing.

However, Roth says that the *Neiye* was far from unique in assigning so much importance to inner cultivation. In fact, he argues that such practices were widespread during the Warring States period and into the Qin and early Han dynasties among the communities of thinkers and practitioners that eventually were identified with the name "Daoist."

In addition to mentioning passages in the *Dao De Jing* and *Zhuang Zi* that reference inner cultivation – some of which I have quoted above – Roth also finds relevant passages in other classics of the 3rd and 2nd centuries BC, such as the *Huai Nan Zi*, the *Annals of Mr Lu*, and other essays in the *Guan Zi* collection, such as *Techniques of the Mind* and *The Purified Mind*.

Roth calls inner cultivation techniques "techniques of the Way" or *dao shu*, and sees them as the defining characteristic of early Daoists more so even than particular intellectual ideas. He argues that "techniques must be seen as a way to define pre-Han intellectual lineages, not just philosophical ideas alone."[17]

He goes on to say:

> "... the 'techniques of the Way' are seen as objective practices that can continue from generation to generation just as can the equally objective measures of the balance beam and water-level. They can continue regardless of whether they are mastered in a given generation..."[18]

In this way, Roth is describing precisely – but possibly without realising it – the theory of patterns transmission that is crucial to the survival and evolution of kung fu. That is the idea that set movements and exercises are passed from master to student, generation after generation, and it is these movements and the principles contained within that define the particular kung fu style.

Ancient Hygienic Practices

Roth also points out that the "techniques of the Way" of the *Neiye* are themselves just links in a longer chain of influence and transmission that join the later post-*Neiye* Daoist practices of yang sheng or "nourishing the vitality or vital principle" with the earlier pre-*Neiye* and even pre-Daoist practices of what he calls "macrobiotic hygiene practitioners":[19] groups of people who practised cultivation with the objective of improving their health and extending their life, as opposed to reaching enlightenment.

Roth quotes Isabelle Robinet, who describes this chain of transmission:

"Yangsheng... the art of 'nourishing the vital principle'... consists of adopting a way of life ruled by physico-mental hygienic principles. This is not specifically a Taoist art and derives from ancient Chinese practices; Taoists adopted, developed and modified them... Even when they seem to be eclipsed by new tendencies, the rules of this art remain a foundation of all Taoist practices in all eras."[20]

This raises the key question of what evidence survives for these ancient pre-Daoist "hygienic" practices.

Roth points out that such practices are mentioned and criticised in chapter 15 of the *Zhuang Zi*:

"To huff and puff, exhale and inhale, blow out the old (breath) and take in the new, do the 'bear stride' and the 'bird-stretch', and to be interested in nothing more than longevity, these are the methods of those who practice the "guiding and pulling (of the vital breath)" (tao-yin...), those who nourish the body (yang-hsing chih Tao...) and try to attain the longevity of Ancestor P'eng."[21]

To put this interesting passage in its due context, it is important to remember that, according to Angus Graham, Chapter 15 was likely added to the *Zhuang Zi* Classic after the time of Zhuang Zi himself, by later so-called Syncretist Daoists in around the 3rd century BC.

Roth goes on to place this fragment in the context of other mentions of similar non-Daoist "hygienic" exercises:

"The tao-yin exercises such as the 'bear stride' and 'bird-stretch' are now known to us through the excavation of a painting at Ma-wangtui and a descriptive text for them at

Chang-chia shan. Chuang Tzu's Syncretist here has in mind both these gymnastic exercises and others involving breath cultivation that are included in such texts as the 'Ten Questions'. That he is criticizing these methods here has as much to do with the fact that they were popular and that he thinks his own are superior as it does with the likely existence of confusion on the part of non-Taoists about how Taoist and physical hygiene techniques differed."[22]

Since all the sources Roth mentioned above are datable to around the 3rd century BC, we can assume with a reasonable level of confidence that, by that stage, physical exercises that were separate from philosophical speculation of Daoists but aimed purely at health and longevity, were popular and widely practised, and there was overlap between these and the inner-cultivation practices such as those of the *Neiye* and other Daoist classics, sufficient that they would see a need to draw distinctions between them.

The 3rd century BC, of course, is later than the likely date for the *Neiye*, but there is also some evidence for these nonphilosophical and pre-Daoist practices from before the *Neiye*. For example, Roth mentions a "Duodecagonal Jade Tablet Inscription on Breath Cultivation" dated to about 400 BC as an early example of breath cultivation practice.[23]

It is an open question how much further back these practices go. My own view is that such breathing and meditation techniques would go back to the trances and medical practices of the shamans, as I mentioned in Chapter 1, though as we are talking about the deepest prehistory before the invention of writing, this can only be speculation on my part.

Apart from its importance for early Daoism, the *Neiye* can also be seen as the missing piece of the puzzle, crucial for the understanding of the connection of classical Daoism of the Warring States, Qin and Han with later Daoist practices down to the present day.

This is the argument made by Russell Kirkland, who explicitly rejects the traditional dichotomy between the classical Daoist

Philosophy, daojia, of Lao Zi and Zhuang Zi, and the later Daoist religion, daojiao, which usually brackets together a number of separate practices such as religious rituals, various heterodox cults, philosophy, external alchemy of potions and amulets, called wai dan, and the internal alchemy, nei dan.

He explains that it is a false dichotomy that was allowed to take root because early Chinese studies in the West were influenced by the Confucian view of Daoism, which found a place for the older classics but rejected anything with physical practice aspects to it as mere superstition.

According to Kirkland, the existence of the *Neiye*, a classic as old as the *Dao De Jing* and the *Zhuang Zi*, proves this view to be mistaken: the inner cultivation practices of nei gong were part of Daoism from the start. It merely continued and branched out into numerous different schools during the Han Dynasty, the Three Kingdoms and the Period of Disunity.[24]

So the picture painted by Roth and Kirkland, which I believe is supported by the emerging textual evidence, is of ancient physical practices, including gymnastics, breathing and meditation, originally practised for their health and longevity benefits, that were at some point in the middle of the first millennium BC taken up by people who would later be called Daoists. These Daoists combined these practices – the dao shu in Roth's terminology, but what I defined under the term nei gong – with some specific philosophical ideas, such as the ones expressed in the *Neiye*, the *Dao De Jing* and the *Zhuang Zi*.

It is this combination of philosophy and practice that I believe was taken up by practitioners of wushu and integrated into their training, initially perhaps for the simple benefits of improving flexibility and strength that the practices offered, but later no doubt for the added efficacy that cultivated qi gave to their martial movements. This blending of wushu and nei gong was precisely what produced the kung fu that we have inherited to the present day.

The evidence so far presented shows us qi practices of the type that survive within kung fu to this day, but it does not pinpoint when exactly this incorporation of nei gong into kung fu first occurred (it may well have been a gradual process that took multiple generations). It also does not yet definitively show that the military and aristocratic classes – i.e. exactly the people who would have practised wushu during that period – took up these cultivation practices. Direct evidence of that came in the Han Dynasty and particularly in the pages of the *Huai Nan Zi*, which will be considered in the next chapter.

Chapter 4

Emergence of Kung Fu during the Han

This chapter looks at a period when the kung fu we know today began to emerge from the mixing of martial skills and Daoist philosophy and practices in the courts of Han kings and aristocrats.

To this day, the Chinese people call themselves "people of the Han" in memory of the great dynasty that ruled China for four hundred years from 202 BC to AD 220.

The Han Dynasty paralleled the Roman Empire on the other side of the Eurasian landmass and was as important in its influence to later Chinese civilisation as the Roman Empire was to later European civilisation.

The Han took over where the Qin left off, expanding the borders of China, strengthening its bureaucracy and developing the idea of the Emperor as the Son of Heaven, responsible for the wellbeing of the people.

After a brief flirtation with Daoist ideas in the early Han as part of the Huang Lao sect (named after its two progenitors Huang Di and Lao Zi, as we have seen), the Han finally settled on Confucianism as the state philosophy of China. They established an early form of state examinations for key officials based on the Five Confucian Classics:

the *Yi Jing*, the *Book of Poetry*, the *Book of Rites*, the *Book of History* and the *Spring and Autumn Annals*.[1]

In military affairs, the Han fought continuously against the barbarian Xiongnu – the Huns portrayed in the Mulan story that is set a little after the Han Dynasty. Under their greatest emperor, Wu Di (156–87 BC), the Han armies pushed the Western border of the Empire past the Great Wall, across the Gobi Desert, all the way to the Tarim Basin in Central Asia, touching the borders of the Classical World conquered by Alexander the Great of Macedonia only a hundred and fifty years earlier.

This conquest opened up the famous Silk Road, enabling trade in silk and porcelain between China and the West. This was how Rome got wind for the first time of the great Empire of the East, and Roman Emperor Marcus Aurelius even sent an envoy across half the globe to pay respects at the Han Court in the year AD 166.[2]

Martial Developments

A significant development during the Han Dynasty which would shape the story of wushu and, by extension, of early kung fu for many centuries to come, was the change in the nature of the Chinese army.

In the early part of the Eastern Han Dynasty, the universal conscription of peasants was abolished. Instead, the business of fighting was left to a small professional army which was supplemented by barbarian troops from nations that paid fealty to the Empire and by convicts forcibly drafted into the army.[3]

This meant that large swathes of the citizens of the Empire became demilitarised and would no longer have had access to either martial arts training or weapons. China was entering an era where martial arts were restricted to specific groups of people: aristocrats, professional soldiers and other specialist groups such as caravan guards and monastery guards made up of lay martial monks (of which Shaolin would be a later famous example).

With martial arts becoming an exclusive practice, the status of its practitioners and teachers would no doubt have greatly increased. Martial arts practice would also likely have become more individual, varied and specialised: a perfect impetus, for example, for the creation of new weapons.

Another key development was the rise of state-sponsored martial arts competitions and demonstrations known as the Hundred Events. These were a development and an elaboration of earlier wrestling and archery competitions but were expanded to include a greater array of weapons, as described by Lorge:

> "...unarmed fighting skills were differentiated. Boxing, which also included kicking and all manner of unarmed striking, was clearly separated from wrestling. There were the "Five Weapons"...: sword, spear, long sword, (ji) halberd, and staff... Archery remained of paramount importance both in war and competition, as well as tripod lifting and the other pure strength exercises."[4]

Histories and encyclopaedias from the Han Dynasty record that for the first time classics were written that were specifically dedicated to the practice of individual martial skills (rather than military strategy). These included the first boxing classic named simply *Boxing* (*Shoubo*) and one of the earliest sword-fencing classics *The Way of the Long Sword*. Unfortunately, neither text has survived the intervening centuries and all we have to go on are brief mentions of them in other works.[5]

Internal Cultivation and Martial Arts

The early Han Dynasty was the period when Daoism established itself both at the Imperial Court and among the general populace. At that time also, there was a rise in practices of nei gong and what is known as internal alchemy, nei dan, whose objective through breathing exercises and meditation was the attainment of immortality and/ or a higher state of being.

These cultivation practices were a direct continuation of the teachings of early Daoist classics such as the *Neiye*, the *Dao De Jing* and the *Zhuang Zi*, mixed in with a whole array of other philosophical and cultural influences such as the ideas of the Five Elements, Yin and Yang and the *Yi Jing*.

The final ingredients added into the mix were the more practical medical techniques of the *Yellow Emperor Classic* and the Daoist gymnastics called daoyin which evolved from the aforementioned longevity exercises practised by the followers of Peng Zu in earlier centuries. Recent archaeological excavations have uncovered more texts explaining these methods dating to the Han Dynasty, including *The Pulling Book* (*Yinshu*) and the *Illustrations of Guiding and Pulling* (*Daoyin tu*). They show an array of exercises, many of them practised from a standing posture and many of them named after animals such as bear, crane, monkey, gibbon, merlin, dragon and turtle.[6]

There seems to have been much overlap in the practice and ideas of different groups, together with competition to find the "right" way of self-cultivation. All together, this broad mix is often referred to as syncretist Daoism.

It is within classics of syncretist Daoism, such as the latter chapters of the *Zhuang Zi* and the *Lie Zi*, that we find the first written evidence of a connection between internal cultivation practices and martial arts, once again in the shape of the then preeminent martial art of archery.

Lorge points out that this is a development of the high esteem in which archery was held by Confucian scholars. However, this time, archery practice was not used as a ritual of propriety, but to develop "a superior, or even superhuman, mental state."[7]

The *Lie Zi* mentions the following exchange between Lie Zi himself and another sage (the same episode is also repeated in the

Zhuang Zi, pointing to a shared source, or perhaps one text influencing the other):

"Lieh-tzu wanted to show off his skill of archery to a friend. He drew his bow and placed a cup of water on his left forearm. Then he notched an arrow and let it fly. Before the first arrow hit the target, he had let off the second and the third. When he saw that all three arrows hit the center of the target, Lieh-tzu was quite pleased with himself. So steady was his hand and so focused was his concentration that the water in the cup did not spill.

"His friend, however, was not impressed. He said to Lieh-tzu, "What you showed me was merely the skill of eye and hand, and not the state of mind of a true archer. Let's go up to the mountains and stand on the edge of a cliff. If you can shoot accurately under these conditions, then I shall be convinced of your mastery in archery."

"The two went up to the mountains, and when they reached the top of a peak, Lieh-tzu's friend walked towards the edge of a cliff that dropped a thousand feet below. Standing with his back to the drop and with half of his foot over the edge, he invited Lieh-tzu to join him.

"Lieh-tzu was already trembling when he saw his friend walk toward the edge of the cliff. Now, at the thought of standing with his back to an abyss, he fell on his face and broke into a cold sweat.

"Lieh-tzu's friend then said, "The master archer can fire an arrow under any condition. Whether he sees the clear sky or faces the yawning abyss, he can still shoot with the same state of mind. He is not affected by conditions of life and death, for nothing can move the stillness of his mind. Look at yourself now. You are so scared that you can't stand up or look straight. How can you even begin to demonstrate the art of archery?"[8]

The language of this text, with its talk of "the stillness of the mind" and being "not affected by conditions of life and death" has clear parallels with the Daoist classics we have already identified as sources of internal cultivation, such as the *Dao De Jing* and the *Neiye*.

The problem with this passage is that we have no idea who wrote it, knowing only that it was not Zhuang Zi and Lie Zi themselves, since scholars such as Angus Graham and Eva Wong point out that the chapters where the passage appears in both were written much later than the supposed lifetimes of the authors.[9] More specifically, we have no idea whether the real authors would have practised a martial art such as archery themselves or just used archery as a useful metaphor.

By the Han Dynasty – unlike the earlier Zhou Dynasty and Warring States times – the expectation that writers and readers of classics would have been aristocrats or members of the knightly class and so would have had at least some training in the martial arts, no longer held true. The needs of a large Empire were driving the professionalization and expansion of the scholarly classes, separate to the aristocracy. This process was only beginning and there would still have been a large overlap between the scholarly and the martial arts trained classes, but the two were no longer one and the same.

We can see, therefore, that to establish the preconditions for the creation of kung fu, it is necessary to show evidence of the aristocratic warrior class having embraced internal practices, and not just scholars. That means we need to demonstrate that texts on internal cultivation were being written by and for the warrior aristocrats, and better still, that such texts were beginning to link up internal cultivation practices with martial arts.

Luckily, there is a classic from this period – arguably the greatest text of syncretist Daoism of them all – in the case of which we can be more certain of the martial inclinations of both its authors and its intended audience. This is the *Huai Nan Zi* classic.

In the pages of the *Huai Nan Zi*, a compendium of syncretist Daoist thought written in the mid-2nd century BC at the court of Liu An, the King of Huai Nan, we have the earliest written evidence of members of the aristocratic warrior class (as the King of Huai Nan and his courtiers certainly were) actively practising internal cultivation and debating concepts such as qi and the Dao.[10]

The text that follows is an example of a passage from the *Huai Nan Zi* that clearly mentions both internal cultivation of qi and physical gymnastic-type exercises (in the context of saying the former is more useful for becoming a sage than the latter):

"Wang Qiao and Chi Songzi blew, vented, exhaled, and inhaled. They purged the old and brought in the new. They left behind their forms and expelled knowledge. They embraced the simple and returned to the genuine so as to wander in the subtle minuteness. Above they penetrated to the cloudy heavens. Now we wish to study their Way. We do not obtain their nourishing of the qi and bringing the spirit to dwell, but we imitate their purging and then inhaling, at the right time crouching, at the right time straightening. That we will be unable to ride the clouds and ascend to greatness is clear indeed."[11]

Regardless of the internal arguments about which type of cultivation – gymnastics or qi cultivation – is more effective, such evidence clearly shows that both were being practised at the time the text was written and were clearly widespread enough among the social group to which the authors themselves belonged to require a comparison and an argument for one over the other.

That the *Huai Nan Zi* was intended for the military classes can be seen from the fact that, among its many chapters on Daoism and cultivation, there is also included a chapter on military strategy, clearly bearing influence both of Daoist ideas and ideas of military strategists such as Sun Zi:

> "In martial arts, it is important that strategy be unfathomable, that form be concealed, and that movements be unexpected, so that preparedness against them be impossible... Only the formless cannot be affected. Sages hide in unfathomability, so their feelings cannot be observed; they operate in formlessness, so their lines cannot be crossed."[12]

This written evidence of cross-fertilisation of martial and Daoist ideas is crucial. It is in such mixed company combining scholarship and martial ability, which existed at the Court of Liu An, that the internal principles of qi and the Dao were most likely to have been incorporated into martial arts practice to create what is now known as kung fu.

Ancient Chinese warriors and hunters of the Shang Dynasty and before may well have taken part in shamanic ceremonies that led them to practise a sort of proto kung fu, but there is no written evidence of this.

Now, however, we not only have the King of Huai Nan commissioning the writing of a Daoist classic, the *Huai Nan Zi*, but Han emperors, such as Han Wudi himself, openly consulting with divines and "immortals" in order to find the means of extending their own lives.[13]

It is clear, therefore, that Daoism and its cultivation techniques were fully embraced by the aristocracy and the ruling classes – i.e. exactly the people who would have been practising martial arts at the highest level – from the Han Dynasty onwards.

This makes it likely that the two practices would have been combined at this time and so supports our theory that kung fu originated in the period between the writing of the *Neiye* and the writing of the *Huai Nan Zi*, i.e. between the 4th and 2nd centuries BC.

Gauging the Weight of Evidence

It has to be said that the evidence provided by the *Huai Nan Zi* is neither definitive nor incontrovertible. It falls some way short of a direct and unambiguous statement about martial artists practising nei gong in order to increase their wushu skills, or exactly how the two practices could have been combined in specific exercises.

It is important, therefore, to be a little cautious before drawing a final conclusion. Scholars such as Lorge and Shahar, for example, have argued that the link between wushu and internal cultivation did not arise until the late Ming and early Qing dynasties, precisely because of a lack of evidence from earlier dynasties.

Both of them have found *some* evidence for this link occurring back in the Warring States–Han period, but deemed it insufficient.

Lorge, as we have already seen, pointed out the connection between archery and self-cultivation in the pages of Confucius' *Analects*, of the *Meng Zi*, and of the *Lie Zi*.[14]

Shahar, meanwhile, quoted from *The Spring and Autumn Annals of Wu and Yue (Wu Yue chunqiu)* from around the 2nd century AD, in which concepts of Yin, Yang, Dao and qi were tied to sword practice, with lines such as:

"The art of swordsmanship is extremely subtle and elusive; its principles are most secret and profound. The Dao has its gate and door, its *yin* and *yang*. Open the gate and close the door; *yin* declines and *yang* rises. When practicing the art of face-to-face combat, concentrate your spirit internally and give the impression of relaxation externally. You should look like a modest woman and strike like a ferocious tiger. As you assume various postures, regulate your *qi*, moving always with the spirit (*shen*)."[15]

Shahar even went as far as to make an exception for sword fencing in his conclusion that there was no link between wushu and self-cultivation until the late Ming:

"The centrality of the sword in Daoist religious practice might have contributed to the incorporation of daoyin gymnastics into fencing. It is likely that as early as the first centuries CE, breathing methods, and possibly even qi-circulation techniques, figured in sword training."[16]

However, neither Lorge nor Shahar seemed aware of each other's evidence on the link with internal cultivation in that pivotal Warring States-Han period – they certainly did not mention it – and neither of them seemed to have surveyed the *Neiye* and the *Huai Nan Zi* as part of the evidence they have considered.

So, from our perspective of seeing all of these different sources together in their totality, does the evidence stack up?

If it were the case that there were numerous other sources of individual martial arts practices (as opposed to military strategy, of which of course there have been many, including the celebrated Sun Zi) surviving from that period but none that directly mention the use of nei gong, then the few indirect mentions in the *Huai Nan Zi*, and elsewhere, would have to be judged as insufficient.

However, Lorge himself, after surveying the available evidence for martial arts practice in early Chinese dynasties, concludes that records about the nature of martial arts being practised in China lack any kind of detail until as late as the Song Dynasty. That is when the earliest surviving classic detailing individual martial skills dates to, namely *The Complete Essentials from the Military Classics (Wujing Zongyao)*.[17] Meanwhile, the earliest written mention of kung fu styles – by General Qi Jiguang[18] – and the earliest mention of internal martial arts – by Huang Zhongxi[19] – do not appear until the Ming Dynasty.

There are two very good reasons for this lack of detailed evidence from before the Song.

The first reason, which both Shahar and Lorge mention, is that before the widespread take-up of wood-block printing during the Ming led to an explosion of literature of every kind, there were simply far fewer books being written and out of them, of course, many would not have survived the passage of time.

The second reason, of which Shahar and Lorge do not take account, is that, during the Song, Ming and Qing dynasties, the literate authors of the various martial arts manuals were exceptional in practising martial arts within their social circle – most literati had nothing to do with martial arts – but during the Warring States and Han period, all aristocrats would have practised martial arts, or at least been taught to do so in their youth, according to Lorge's own account. That could well explain why there is so little specific mention of martial arts practices in that period: how often do we devote time describing in a manual something that everyone already knows and practises, particularly at a time when writing is a rarity?

Only by failing to appreciate both of these reasons can it be concluded that an abundance of manuals in the Ming and Qing dynasties, and a lack of them in the Han Dynasty, is proof of anything.

Against the background of a general lack of detailed evidence of any kind about individual martial arts practice earlier than the Song and Ming period, the mentions in the *Huai Nan Zi*, the *Lie Zi* and *The Spring and Autumn Annals of Yue and Wu* suddenly look far more significant than would appear at first glance. We have only a few mentions of wushu and nei gong together, but that is out of the total number of sources on wushu that is itself very small, so proportionately the evidence is not insignificant.

Without further texts emerging from archaeological digs, as happened with Mawangdui, the evidence we have in front of us is probably as good as we can expect to get, so I feel comfortable in dating the emergence of kung fu as the synthesis between wushu and nei gong to this period.

We should also be mindful of the problems with the opposite argument made by Lorge, that internal cultivation and daoyin gymnastics were not practised together with the martial arts until the middle of the Ming Dynasty.

That would mean that the same group of people, first the aristocrats of the Warring States, Qin and Han periods, and then the literati of later dynasties, practised martial arts and nei gong side by side for over one-and-a-half thousand years, and connected both in their writings such as the *Lie Zi* and *Huai Nan Zi* passages quoted above, but did not think to mix the two in practice, did not think to use the meditation exercises to calm their minds in battle, and did not use the breathing exercises to give strength to their movements. To me, this seems unlikely.

In Part 2, I will attempt to trace the development of both martial arts and internal cultivation after the Han Dynasty, and show how they parallel each other, often drawing from the same developments in the wider Chinese culture.

Part 2

Development and Maturity

Chapter 5

Three Kingdoms and the Rise of the Alchemists

The Three Kingdoms and the Period of Disunity that followed was a time of war and chaos, but it produced some of the greatest fighters in Chinese history and at the same time some of its most famous alchemists and Daoist immortals.

After four centuries of strong centralised rule, the Han Empire that had given Chinese people their name (the Han, or Han Chinese) started to weaken. Towards the end of the 2nd century AD, the imperial court had a succession of young and weak emperors who came under the dominance of their eunuch advisors. A number of rival warlords saw the opportunity to take over.

After a short period of all-against-all struggle, the Empire split into three rival kingdoms: the Wei kingdom in the north under Cao Cao and his descendants, the Shu Han kingdom in the southwest under Liu Bei, who claimed to be a distant relative of the Han royal family, and the Wu kingdom in the south, under Sun Quan.

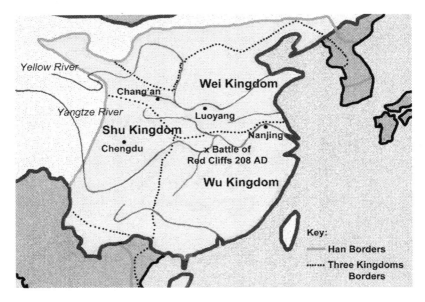

Map 2: Han Dynasty and Three Kingdoms

The Three Kingdoms Novel and Reality

These three rival kingdoms vied with each other for eighty years, giving the name Three Kingdoms to that short but celebrated period in Chinese history. It was immortalised by the author Luo Guan-zhong (c. 1330–1400) in his novel *Romance of the Three Kingdoms*, though the novel was written much later – in the 14th century – from older oral traditions.

To this day, Chinese people see the Three Kingdoms period as the height of chivalry and romance and revere the names of its key characters: Liu Bei, Guan Yu and Zhang Fei, the three brothers of the Peach Orchard, the strategist Zhuge Liang, and their rivals, Cao Cao, Sun Quan, Zhou Yu of Red Cliff fame, and Sima Yi.

They are known by every Chinese man and woman as semi-myth-ical heroes, with Guan Yu in particular still venerated across China as the God of War and the patron saint of both martial artists and scholars, the latter because of his love for the Confucian Classics.[1] Remarkably, however, historians have shown that the main characters of the stories listed above were all based on real people.

Chivalrous this period may have been, but it was also extremely bloody, with what was in effect a civil war ebbing and flowing almost continuously for eighty years. During this period, the population of China plummeted, from 56 million in AD 157 to 16 million in AD 280.[2]

Although much of that drop can be accounted for by the difficulty of counting households during a time of war and chaos, it is likely that millions of people died in the wars and the epidemics that accompanied them.[3]

The character of Cao Cao certainly suited his times well. Notorious for his saying "Better to wrong the world, than have it wrong me,"[4] he has been remembered in history as the epitome of ruthlessness and cunning, though no doubt an inspirational and charismatic leader of his men.

To this day, Chinese people educated in the classics argue about whether it was Cao Cao who was responsible for the chaos in his attempts to bring the Empire under control, or whether it was in fact the noble Liu Bei who, through resisting the fall of the Han Dynasty, prolonged the period of chaos and paid the price in the blood of his friends and followers, only to delay but not avert the inevitable. I remember a long, fun and inebriated night debating this very point with a kung fu master in Shandong, my Chinese improving with every cup of bai jiu!

Regardless of who ultimately won or lost, both history and popular memory recorded the key protagonists of this drama as martial artists of unparalleled skill, showing the full range of talents in wushu, military strategy, generalship and, quite possibly, the new internal cultivation practices developed by the masters of the *Neiye* and the *Huai Nan Zi* a few centuries earlier.

Historical records of that period note that the practice of war during the Three Kingdoms period reserved an important place for duels between champions of rival armies in exactly the way the stories portray. Figures such as Guan Yu, Zhang Fei and Lu Bu were fighters in the mould of individual champions, unlike Liu Bei, Cao Cao and Zhuge Liang, who were more famous for their strategy and leadership than their individual skill at arms.

It seems the Three Kingdoms period was a combination of the large-scale strategy-based warfare practised during the Warring States period and warfare that relied on individual champions testing each other's skill, which was more a feature of the preceding Zhou Dynasty.

One very concrete legacy of this kind of champion-on-champion fighting was the creation of many of the famous weapons that are still in use in martial arts today, including the Guan Dao and Snake Spear, made famous by Guan Yu and Zhang Fei respectively.

Large and heavy weapons of this type are clearly of little use to a normal soldier fighting in regimental lines, but of great value for their reach and shear killing power to individual champions testing their skills against each other and able to fight out of formation.

Zhuge Liang and Internal Cultivation

The character of Zhuge Liang is particularly interesting as far as our definition of kung fu is concerned. In the novel, he is described as a Daoist who cut himself off from the world for the purposes of self-cultivation, before being persuaded to join the war by Liu Bei. On becoming Liu Bei's chief minister, Zhuge Liang applied the insights and the arcane skills given to him by his cultivation practices to become an unrivalled military strategist, able single-handedly to turn the tide of battles.

The two sides of his nature, being both a Daoist sage and a military strategist, recall nothing so clearly as the passage of the *Huai Nan Zi* we quoted earlier, which described the Daoist interpretation of *The Art of War*.

The very fact, if true, that such a character as Zhuge Liang could be both a Daoist and a military leader during this period, with no hint of conflict or contradiction between his two roles, fits in well with our theory that kung fu as the blending of wushu and Daoist internal cultivation was already well established at this time.

We have to be aware, however, that many of the sources that describe what characters such as Zhuge Liang were like dated from centuries after the actual historical events and other sources, including the ones *The Romance of Three Kingdoms* was based on, were transmitted only orally down the generations.

From H.C. Tillman's review of how the portrayal of Zhuge Liang's personality, alleged Daoism or Confucianism, and his ability as a general and a strategist changed over the centuries depending on which source you consult, it is clear that we cannot trust the novel's portrayal as being in any way more authoritative than others.[5]

However, unlike with the story of Yue Nu we quoted in Chapter 1, which was similarly based on legends and traditions which could not be verified, we at least have the benefit of many other writings that *can* be dated accurately to the period of the Three Kingdoms and shortly afterwards. These describe scholars and members of the aristocracy doing the kind of things that the oral histories ascribed to Zhuge Liang, as we shall see when we consider the figures of Hua Tuo and Ge Hong later on.

So, although we cannot be certain that the historical Zhuge Liang practised internal cultivation in the way oral histories and the novel describe, we can be certain that some of his contemporaries did. It is not beyond the realms of possibility, then, that the oral traditions may actually have had a kernel of truth in them.

The Period of Disunity

Following the short and bloody interlude of the Three Kingdoms period, the course of history took China into three hundred years of political chaos known as the Period of Disunity, during which northern China was invaded by the Toba Wei, a nomadic tribe related to the Mongols, and both northern and southern China went through a quick succession of dozens of short-lived dynasties, some indigenous (particularly in the south) and some not.

This makes it sound like the Dark Ages for Chinese civilisation, but actually this period also saw a flowering of culture, including poetry and art, and the establishment of both Daoism and Buddhism as key religions with millions of adherents, as the Chinese people took solace from political chaos in spiritual and artistic pursuits.

So, unlike a similar period of disruption in Western Europe after the fall of the Roman Empire, the Chinese civilisation did not splinter or fade away. Instead, each new dynasty, including those under the rule of the Toba Wei "barbarians", simply carried on with the structures and institutions of the past.

This is a key feature of Chinese history, often remarked upon by historians: China has incredible resilience as a civilisation and each new wave of conquerors inevitably end by being swallowed up by the host culture, given enough time.

The Rise of Daoist Alchemy

From the 3rd century AD and through the Period of Disunity, we have increasing evidence for Daoist nei gong cultivation, meditation practices, breathing exercises and the rise of internal and external alchemy, nei dan and wai dan.

Two key examples that show obvious influence of practices such as those in the *Neiye* and the non-philosophical "hygiene" school of Peng Zu are the early Daoists Hua Tuo (c. AD 140–208) and Ge Hong (AD 283–343), whose name is perhaps better known under the spelling of Ko Hung.

Hua Tuo was a famous physician and supposed Daoist immortal, mentioned in *The Romance of the Three Kingdoms*, who invented a moving qi gong based on capturing the essence of five animals: bear, tiger, deer, ape and bird, in what has often been taken in martial arts literature as the earliest verifiable evidence of both internal styles (a possible precursor to Ba Gua and Tai Ji) and animal styles (a possible precursor to southern styles such as Monkey, Tiger and Crane).

Having explored the earlier evidence, we can now see of course that Hua Tuo did not invent something completely new, for bear and bird exercises were mentioned in, among other places, the latter chapters of the *Zhuang Zi*, dating to four hundred years before Hua Tuo lived.

More likely is that Hua Tuo built on earlier "hygiene" and longevity exercises – and before even that on prehistoric shamanic spirit possessions and spirit dances, where the shaman assumes the qualities of a particular beast – in developing his animal forms and, by making them famous, he served as an important link from ancient practices into more recent qi gong and kung fu styles of medieval China.

Ge Hong meanwhile is famous to this day as an early practitioner of both internal alchemy of qi cultivation and the external alchemy of elixirs and potions, penning the great alchemical classic the *Bao Pu Zi (Pao-p'u-tzu)*.

He was one of the great popularisers of the whole quest of becoming an immortal, which dominated later Daoism and also influenced the more magical and romantic side of martial arts practice in China, including the wuxia romances of martial arts heroes and secret cults that have provided so much source material to Hong Kong cinema. The next time you see a martial arts immortal performing magical feats on the silver screen, you will know that to some small degree it was influenced by the old alchemist Ge Hong, who, like Hua Tuo, was also said to have become an immortal himself.

On a more serious note, however, scholars such as Kirkland point out just how many parallels there are between Ge Hong's internal alchemy and the internal cultivation of the much older *Neiye*, demonstrating a clear chain of cultural transmission, which Kirkland argued then continued through the *Bao Pu Zi's* influence on later alchemists, Daoists and qi gong practitioners.[6]

These parallels can clearly be seen from the following extract from the *Bao Pu Zi*:

"It is hoped that those who nourish life will learn extensively and comprehend the essential, gather whatever there is to see and choose the best. It is not sufficient to depend on cultivating only one thing. It is also dangerous for people who love life to rely on their own specialty. Those who know the techniques of the *Classic of the Mysterious Lady* and the *Classic of the Plain Lady* [books on sexual regimen no longer extant] will say that only the 'art of the chamber' will lead to salvation. Those who understand the method of breathing exercises will say that only the permeation of the vital power can prolong life. Those who know the method of stretching and bending will say that only physical exercise can prevent old age. And those who know the formulas of herbs will say that only medicine will make life unending. They fail in their pursuit of Tao because they are so onesided. People of superficial knowledge think they have enough when they happen to know of only one way and do not realize that the true seeker will search unceasingly even after he has acquired some good formulas."[7]

Ge Hong here helpfully summarises all the practices that were seen as effective means to reach immortality in the 3rd and 4th centuries AD. We can see that the two practices we first encountered in the 4th century BC and which we argued in the last couple of chapters were precursors to kung fu – physical gymnastics and breathing exercises of qi gong – are still very much part of the post-Han world. In addition to them are listed two newer ways to achieve sagehood: sexual regimens that were a staple feature of internal alchemy, nei dan, and finally the external alchemy, wai dan, of herbs and potions.

Phases of Development of Internal Cultivation

There is a clear line of transmission of internal cultivation practice over the period of seven hundred years between the writing of the *Neiye* and the *Bao Pu Zi*.

If we go outside the reach of written evidence, we can hypothesise an even longer chain stretching back past the *Neiye* to earlier shamanic practices and then going forwards in time via the *Bao Pu Zi* to the qi gong and kung fu practices of today.

I would bracket the prehistoric shamanic practices and the ancient health and longevity exercises such as the daoyin, which developed from them, as the First Phase of self-cultivation. Arising in Chinese prehistory and stretching into the Zhou Dynasty, it was in this period that early internal cultivation techniques may have first merged with indigenous Chinese martial practices to become a kind of proto kung fu. As discussed in Chapter 1, this can only be a hypothesis because of the lack of written records surviving from this early period.

The Second Phase of internal cultivation we can define with more certainty. It was the period from the Warring States to the early Han Dynasty, when the ancient health and longevity exercises were enriched by philosophical ideas to become the nei gong cultivation practices of classics such as the *Neiye* and the *Huai Nan Zi*, which later became integral to Daoism.

The final, Third Phase of internal cultivation, stretching from the late Han Dynasty to the modern day, saw the rise of nei dan, internal alchemy, and wai dan, external alchemy, practices, the early examples of which included the alchemy of Ge Hong.

All these practices saw continual development over centuries, sometimes running in parallel as distinct streams, but always borrowing from each other. In this way they gave rise over time to hundreds of different styles and disciplines, some Daoist, some Buddhist or Confucian, and others not connected to religion at all, including the cultivation techniques present in the many styles of kung fu and qi gong today.

This allows us to understand the way that disciplines that are still being practised now are not unique and self-contained but are a natural extension of ancient Chinese traditions.

The Arrival of Buddhism

Buddhism was also an important if late influence in the area of internal cultivation. It was towards the end of the Period of Disunity, in the 5th century, that the Shaolin Monastery was established on Songshan in Henan Province, a mountain range that had already been sacred to Daoists for seven hundred years before that.[8] And it was in the 6th century, during the reign of Emperor Liang Wudi, that Bodhidharma arrived in China and, according to legend, meditated for nine years in a cave on Songshan, famously facing a bare wall, before, supposedly, teaching the monks his own variant of breathing and energy exercises.

The story of Bodhidharma teaching the monks is perhaps the most famous and widely quoted theory about the origin of kung fu: that it was invented in the Shaolin Monastery in the 6th century AD.

This Shaolin kung fu origin theory is based largely on the evidence of the existence of two classics ascribed to Bodhidharma: *The Bone Marrow Washing Classic, Ba Duan Jing*, and *The Sinew Metamorphosis Classic, Yi Jin Jing*, both of which deal with internal cultivation, which was claimed by Shaolin monks to be at the root of what made their martial arts distinctive.

At first glance, therefore, Shaolin would seem to have met our criterion of marrying together martial skill and internal qi cultivation, necessary for the practice to be accepted as kung fu, as far back as the 6th century AD, and it seems to have clearer evidence to corroborate it than the *Huai Nan Zi*.

However, this is entirely based on the dating of the two classics to the time of Bodhidharma himself. This has been disputed by scholars, from the celebrated martial arts historian, Tang Hao (1887–1959), to such present generation scholars as Meir Shahar. Indeed, Shahar follows Tang Hao in dating the *Yi Jin Jing*, as the earliest of the two classics, to the year 1624, and argues that it was likely written outside the Shaolin Monastery by one Master Zongheng from Mount Tiantai, who was likely a Daoist rather than a Buddhist.[9]

This still makes the *Yi Jin Jing* the "earliest extant handbook that integrates daoyin [Daoist gymnastics] and quan [open-hand fighting]"[10] explicitly, but that is almost two thousand years after the admittedly less direct but nonetheless compelling references in such classics as the *Huai Nan Zi*.

Just because the two classics do not appear to have been written until the late Ming Dynasty, it does not mean that some sort of internal cultivation was not practised by Shaolin monks much earlier on. After all, Buddhism originated in India, where there is a long history of native Indian internal cultivation in the form of yoga.

Indeed, there is one piece of tantalising evidence connecting the Shaolin Monastery, kung fu and internal cultivation to the 6th century. Meir Shahar includes a Tang-period anecdote written by Zhang Zhuo (ca. 660–741) about a Shaolin monk by the name of Sengchou (480–560) who was both a famous practitioner of meditation and also seems to have practised some kung fu-like exercises.[11]

According to the anecdote, when Sengchou arrived at the Shaolin Monastery as a novice, he was weak and was bullied by the other novices who always beat him in wrestling. In despair, Sengchou asked the Buddhist deity Vajrapani to gift him strength. After six days of continuous prayer, Vajrapani relented and granted his wish via the unusual means of forcing him to eat "sinews-flesh", forbidden to a Buddhist monk.

Sengchou emerged changed from his experience, at which point the story picks up:

"The Dhyana Master [i.e. Sengchou; Dhyana means "meditation" in Buddhist terminology] said: "I have strength now. I suspect not the same kind as yours." Then he flexed his arms, revealing his powerful sinews and bones. He looked practically like a god.

"Before they recovered their senses, the Dhyana Master said, "I will give you a demonstration," whereupon he entered the hall and started walking horizontally on the walls. He advanced first from the east, then from the west, a total of several hundred feet. Then he leaped upwards, his head hitting the ceiling-beams several times. Finally he lifted several thousand pounds. His fighting was swift and powerful.

"Those who belittled him prostrated themselves on the ground, their sweat trickling. No one dared face up to him."[12]

Wall running, leaping, lifting weights and fighting, are, of course, all old favourites in the Shaolin training regimen, as well as that of many other styles of kung fu, to this day. Shahar points out the interesting parallels with later Shaolin kung fu, wondering if this is the earliest evidence of that style's existence.[13] But he fails to point out something that is almost as interesting: that, since the monk Sengchou was a historical figure, famous for his meditation skills, this anecdote can also be taken as evidence of the mixing of kung fu and internal cultivation practices, of which meditation formed a key part.

I would argue that evidence from anecdotes such as these and the later Shaolin classics of internal cultivation, the *Ba Duan Jing* and the *Yi Jin Jing,* show Shaolin monks, at most, *developing* the cultivation ideas of far earlier classics such as the *Neiye* and the *Huai Nan Zi,* and the later Daoist teachings of figures such as Hua Tuo and Ge Hong, rather than inventing them from scratch. There is a continuum here, in which Shaolin has its place alongside others both before and after them.

We can see, therefore, that Shaolin cannot be said to have invented kung fu, not even in the narrower sense of adding internal cultivation to the older Chinese wushu to make it into a kung fu practice. This is not to denigrate the importance that the beginnings of cultivation practice in Shaolin would have on the later history of kung fu, which, as I will argue in future chapters, was indeed significant.

Chapter 6

The Golden Age

This chapter covers the Golden Age of Chinese civilisation, when kung fu reached the zenith of its influence and many of the oldest styles still practised today, such as Shaolin and Wudang, are traditionally said to have been created.

The Tang Dynasty was founded in AD 618 by Li Yuan (566–635), after the short-lived Sui Dynasty did the hard work of reuniting China but then collapsed from the strains caused by its own achievement. Li Yuan was there to pick up where the Sui left off.

The Tang Dynasty was hugely important for the further development of kung fu because its emperors gave their personal patronage to both Daoist internal cultivation practices and to martial arts.

This allowed both practices to reach a much wider following among the aristocracy, the military, the scholar bureaucrats and the growing religious community. The direct consequence of this was the creation of some of the most celebrated styles, weapons and fighting methods of kung fu that survive to the present day.

The Three Emperors

Li Yuan was a skilled general and administrator, but he was outshone in both areas by his son Li Shimin (599–649), who, after helping his father fight off their rivals and establish the dynasty, eventually took over as the second emperor under the reign name Taizong and left his mark on history as one of the greatest rulers China had ever seen. He rebuilt China as a powerful empire once again, matching and even exceeding the extent of the Han Empire, including by once again pushing the Chinese borders westwards along the Silk Road into Central Asia.

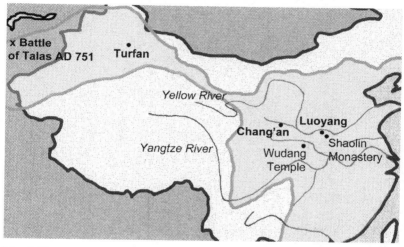

Map 3: Tang Dynasty

In fact, the early Tang Dynasty was blessed with not one but three truly great emperors. In addition to Taizong, his own concubine Wu Zetian (c. 625–705) became China's first and only female emperor, temporarily interrupting the Tang Dynasty to ascend the Throne of Heaven herself as founder of the Zhou Dynasty (this "Zhou" written differently in Chinese script to its predecessor). Wu Zetian quite deliberately used the masculine title of "emperor" rather than the feminine "empress" to underline the fact that she was in power in her own right, which scandalised the traditionalists at court.

However, Wu Zetian was every bit as ruthless as Cao Cao and brooked no opposition. While still a concubine, she had her rival, the wife of Emperor Taizong, killed, then imprisoned her own sons, whom she thought too weak and ineffectual to rule. She crushed any hint of rebellion against her and it is only in the last year of her life, when she was eighty and assailed by the frailties of age, that the officials and her disenfranchised sons found the courage to overthrow her regime, imprisoning her supporters and executing the two young brothers she had kept as her pet lovers. She abdicated and died soon after.[1]

The final member of the triumvirate was Emperor Xuanzong (685–762), Wu Zetian's grandson, under whose nearly fifty-year reign China is thought to have achieved its absolute zenith of power, wealth and artistic achievement.

Poetry, Religion and Influence on Japan

During the reign of Emperor Xuanzong, the Tang Dynasty produced China's two greatest poets, chief among them, Li Bai (701–762) and Du Fu (713–768), not to mention countless other artists whose works are treasured to this day.[2]

Tang poetry was considered one of the select number of arts that were essential for every gentleman to master, the others being music, calligraphy, painting, playing the weiqi and kung fu. Li Bai, for example, was famous for his straight sword fighting in addition to his talent for poetry.

The Tang also produced some of the greatest religious thinkers, including the monk Xuanzang (c. 596–664) – who travelled to India and back in search of original sutras and who inspired the famous novel *Journey to the West* – and the monk Huineng (638–713), the Sixth Patriarch of Chan Buddhism and a direct line successor of Bodhidharma at Shaolin Monastery.

Although Confucianism was still seen as the official religion of the state, the Tang Dynasty also gave imperial patronage to Daoists, since the family name of the Tang Emperors, "Li," was supposedly the same as that of Lao Zi. The real reason, however, was that Daoism was very popular among the literati at the time and the Tang

Emperors sought to use its popularity to legitimise themselves. Such legitimisation, of course, was useful for both parties, and Daoist priests and alchemists flocked to the Tang Court in great numbers. Such celebrated Daoist masters as Sima Chengzhen (646–735) and Du Guangting (850–933) even acted as advisors and teachers of Tang Emperors.[3]

The relationship between the Tang Emperors and Buddhists was more mixed. Wu Zetian was a great Buddhist patron but many other Emperors were anti-Buddhist and in the latter part of the dynasty there was official persecution against this religion, although particular temples and monasteries, like Shaolin, were protected.[4]

It was in Shaolin Monastery that Chan Buddhism truly came into its own with the instalment of the Sixth Patriarch, Huineng, who is seen as both the author of the key Chan text, the *Platform Sutra*, and the founder of the southern branch of Chan Buddhism, which was fated to have the greatest influence both in China and in Japan, where it would be transmitted by Huineng's disciples.

It has been argued that Chan Buddhism borrowed much from native Daoist traditions[5] and it is certainly the case that Chan Buddhism, like Daoism, put a lot of emphasis on internal cultivation practices, including breathing techniques and sitting meditation, now known universally by its Japanese name: Za Zen. I have also already noted in Chapter 2 that the *Zhuang Zi* is seen as a key text for Chan Buddhism, despite being a Daoist classic.

This crucial connection between Buddhism and Daoism ensured that Buddhist styles of kung fu still had the benefit of Daoist nei gong practices and did not develop down a different path. As mentioned in the Introduction, today all styles, Buddhist or Daoist, contain the crucial element of internal cultivation of qi that makes them kung fu.

It was during the Tang Dynasty and the following Song Dynasty that Chinese influence spread across East and Southeast Asia, to Korea, Japan and Vietnam, bringing with it the Chinese script, the three great religions of Confucianism, Daoism and Buddhism, as well as cuisine, dress, tea cultivation and weapons technology.

To this day, a trip to see the cultural highlights of Kyoto or Nara in Japan acts much like a journey back in time to the culture of Tang China, so influential was it and so treasured by Japan that its arts and traditions have been preserved and developed to perfection in the classical Japanese aesthetic of bonsai trees, kimonos, sumo wrestling, tea ceremonies, rock gardens and Buddhist shrines, paintings and porcelain, all of which draw inspiration from the Tang Dynasty and its successor, the Song Dynasty.[6]

In this way, Tang China's influence in Asia was much like the influence of Classical Greece and Rome on modern European culture, on the design of our own buildings, the shape of our letters and the direction of our thought.

Wars and Rebellions

Between the years AD 650 and 750, Tang China was probably the most powerful country in the world. Its only real rival would have been the Abbasid Caliphate, with the court of Caliph Harun Al Rashid a few decades later every bit as blessed with both power and art as that of Emperor Xuanzong.

When the Abbasid and Tang empires came into contact with each other at the battle of Talas in AD 751, the Chinese army was defeated, mainly because its supply line was overextended a thousand miles from the centre of its own empire, but the consequences of that battle were far greater than just a check on China's western expansion.

During the battle, the Islamic army captured a master papermaker and, through him, the West discovered the secret of paper-making, which would spark a revolution in knowledge, first in the Islamic world and then, via the contacts between Christianity and Islam, in Western Europe as well.

Paper was actually not invented by the Tang, but by the Han Dynasty, six hundred years earlier, but there were a whole host of technological inventions that were first created during the Tang Dynasty, not least the secret of gunpowder and the technology of block printing.

The growth of Tang China came to a juddering halt in the middle of the 8th century when the An Lushan rebellion almost toppled the Empire. This followed hard on the heels of the loss of the Tarim Basin after the Battle of Talas and an almost simultaneous invasion of Western China by Tibetan forces.

If a single episode can sum up all these misfortunes, it is the flight of the elderly Emperor Xuanzong from his own capital, under threat by An Lushan's rebels. The Emperor's courtesan Yang Guifei was partly responsible for the An Lushan debacle, as An was her adopted son and achieved the prominence that allowed him to rebel thanks largely to her patronage and her influence over the Emperor's heart.

As Xuanzong fled westwards from the rebels, his retreat was cut off by a unit of Tibetan troops. Faced with the double threat ahead of them and behind, the Emperor's own courtiers rebelled against him and forced the old man to sacrifice Yang Guifei, whom all held to blame, before they would follow him any further.

With a breaking heart, Xuanzong had no choice but to comply and Guifei was strangled with a silk cord in an act later immortalised by the great poet Bai Juyi (772—846) in his poem *The Everlasting Wrong*. So closed the reign of one of China's most illustrious emperors.[7]

The Tang Empire was sufficiently powerful to survive all these misfortunes and would last for another hundred and fifty years, but it never had the same sense of confidence and creative energy thereafter. Instead, it was a long period of decline that finally led to the end of the dynasty in the year AD 907.

However, even when it collapsed, its cultural legacy and the structures of state that the dynasty put in place were strong enough that the period of chaos was relatively short-lived. Another dynasty, the Song, picked up the torch in AD 960, and in many ways, for its first hundred and fifty years, the Song Dynasty turned the clock back to the glory days of the High Tang.

Trade and culture again picked up and the Song produced some of the greatest works of art in Chinese history, achieving the same heights in the field of watercolour painting, for example, as the Tang did in poetry.

The Shaolin Connection

From its very start, the story of the Tang Dynasty was tied to the story of kung fu.

In the year 621, Li Shimin, the future Emperor Taizong, was given military assistance by a group of Shaolin warrior monks during one of the early battles for the throne.

This intervention by Shaolin monks was no accident, as the Monastery and its lands were located in a militarily strategic location, close to the capital Luoyang and controlling one of the approaches to that city.[8]

When General Wang Shichong made a rival claim for the throne, he quickly occupied Luoyang. In the process of that occupation, he forcibly took over the Cypress Valley Estate (Baigu Zhuang) which belonged to the Shaolin Monastery. Just as Li Shimin massed his troops to encircle and blockade Luoyang, the Shaolin monks must have judged the time propitious to launch their own attack and, in one swoop, both regain their estate and get in the good books of what by that time looked like the likely winning side of the dynastic conflict.[9]

As the result of successfully pushing out Wang's troops from the Cypress Valley Estate, when Li Shimin ascended the throne, the Shaolin Monastery was given a number of privileges by royal decree, including military titles for the monks involved in the Emperor's rescue and confirmation of their ownership of the Cypress Valley Estate itself, which was happily recorded by the monks on a number of stelae that still survive within the grounds of the Monastery.[10]

This royal connection laid the foundation for great wealth and power for the Monastery, and no doubt the martial fame so gained by the Monastery later encouraged the development of kung fu practice there. However, as both Lorge and Shahar point out, there is precious little evidence that a specific Shaolin kung fu was already practised at the Monastery in Tang times. Certainly none of the many official visitors to the Monastery who have left records of what they have seen there mention kung fu practice prior to the Ming Dynasty seven hundred years later.[11]

Shahar is sympathetic to at least the possibility of Shaolin kung fu being developed before the Ming Dynasty. As evidence, he quotes the story of the monk Sengchou, written during the Tang Dynasty, as we have already seen in Chapter 5, and he also points out that, in the first records of outside visitors seeing Shaolin kung fu being practised, dated to the Ming Dynasty, those visitors said that what they saw was not recently developed, but rather had been practised by the monks for centuries prior to their visit.[12]

Lorge, however, is more sceptical and points out that Shaolin, as a significant and wealthy landowner, would no doubt have employed guards, and many of its monks may well have been ex-military men who later retired to the Monastery as was the fashion during the Tang Dynasty. Either or both sources of men with martial skills could have provided the Monastery with the men to conduct its raid on the Cypress Valley Estate, without that being proof that a separate Shaolin kung fu was being practised in the Monastery.[13]

My own instinct falls somewhere in between these two positions. If, as Lorge speculates, military men may have retired to the Monastery, then it is likely that they would have been given tasks commensurate with their past experiences, such as overseeing the guards the Monastery would have needed to employ to protect its lands. And if guards were employed, then some would have likely converted to Buddhism and been accepted as novice monks. In this way, there was plenty of opportunity for blurring the lines between use of martial arts *by* the Monastery and practice of martial arts *in* the Monastery. The likelihood is that some kung fu was practised but it may not yet have been uniquely Shaolin kung fu. Without further sources being identified, however, none of this can be fully resolved, but that would be my hypothesis.

The Explosion of Martial Arts during the Song Dynasty

Outside of Shaolin, kung fu styles were being created and popularised at an unprecedented pace, particularly during the Song Dynasty, due to the growing popularity of martial arts demonstrations in the entertainment quarters of the capital and other big cities.[14]

Using martial arts for demonstration purposes has always been a feature of practice, stretching back as far as written record allows us to see, with martial dances and the Han Dynasty's One Hundred Events. During the Tang Dynasty, sword dances were very popular at court and elsewhere[15] but during the Song, the scale and variety increased dramatically.

> "[In the entertainment quarter] a wide variety of martial arts was performed purely to entertain an audience: boxing, wrestling, archery (with bow and crossbow), fencing, sword dances, and so on. The men and women who performed there were professional martial artists expert in particular fighting skills. These martial arts would have grown out of both the fighting techniques of the military and the arts practiced locally all over the empire... The circulation of martial artists was promoted by these performances, as artists could now travel and perform as a regular entertainment, just like other services. This actually emphasized regional variation since different ways of fighting was [sic] an attraction. Whereas the martial arts in the army were constantly regularized and made uniform throughout all the units to the greatest extent possible... performance martial arts required differences to be maintained and promoted."[16]

We see, therefore, the emergence of the culture of travelling martial arts competitors, teachers and performers that would continue in China into the 20th century. Kung fu was now becoming a trade separate from service in the military, though of course there would always have been overlap between the two, as retired soldiers no doubt used their martial skills to make a living for themselves in such performances, while the best civilian martial artists would have been offered a route into the army via the official military exam system, as we shall see.

The Song period is supposedly when the Daoist Wudang Quan, the ancestor of internal styles such as Tai Ji, was established. According to legend its originator was the immortal Zhang Sanfeng, who kept appearing in the written records over a span of a few centuries, from the Song Dynasty to the Ming.

Regardless of whether there is a grain of truth in these legends, certainly the Wudang Daoist Temple, which would later develop close connections with Wudang Quan, was in existence from the Tang period onwards.

Also, the Tang Dynasty was the high watermark for internal alchemy, or nei dan, texts, as those practices were considered an important part of an enlightened man's life and were very popular among scholars and aristocrats at the Tang Court, so Daoist internal cultivation was certainly widely practised at the time.[17]

As such, the preconditions for an evolution of an internal style around the Wudang Temple were there, however there is no written evidence of Wudang Quan's existence in the Tang Dynasty. In fact, Lorge points out that the first verifiable written reference to an internal style of any kind was the epitaph to the Ming Dynasty martial artist called Wang Zhengnan (1617–1669) written by Huang Zongxi in 1669:

"Shaolin is famous for its boxers. However, its techniques are chiefly offensive, which creates opportunities for an opponent to exploit. Now there is another school that is called "internal," which overcomes movement with stillness. Attackers are effortlessly repulsed. Thus we distinguish Shaolin as "external.""

"The Internal School was founded by Zhang Sanfeng of the Song Dynasty, Sanfeng was a Daoist alchemist of the Wudang Mountains. He was summoned by Emperor Huizong of the Song, but the road was impassable. That night he dreamt that the God of War transmitted the art of boxing to him and the following morning [he] single-handedly killed over a hundred bandits."[18]

If we take the dating of Zhang Sanfeng's creation of Wudang Quan to the reign of Emperor Huizong at face value, then it must have been created between 1101, when Huizong ascended the throne, and 1125, when he abdicated. Beyond that, however, it is impossible to be certain.

Armies and Weapons

Sword fighting was important in Tang China in two very different ways. On the battlefield, the single-edged dao broadsword had fully replaced the jian straight sword by this time and had become a key weapon for Chinese armies, a position of pre-eminence it would maintain all the way through to the Qing Dynasty. At court, on the other hand, literati and officials favoured the jian straight sword precisely because it was no longer seen as a weapon of the soldier but rather as "the elegant weapon of a cultivated man"[19] and one that connected the Literati that practised with the jian with their ancestors back in the Han and Qin dynasties.

Interestingly, the early form of the famous katana sword, which was later brought to new heights of perfection by Japanese masters, was actually first developed in Tang and Song China:

"Although these [early straight chokuto type] swords were made in Japan, they were mere imitations of Chinese blades. High-ranking officers usually carried expensive swords made in China... This imitation of the Chinese sword was gradually developed into the typical samurai sword."[20]

The same was true of the design of lacquer armour we now associate with Japanese samurai, which was based on similar armour worn by Chinese warriors.

Tang armies relied on cavalry armed with swords, bows and lances, and on infantry armed with swords, bows, spears and different kinds of polearm. The crossbow was less prominent in Tang armies than it was under the Han, though it became very important again during the Song Dynasty.[21]

The officer class was mostly aristocratic in origin, and to achieve high rank they took "examinations placing emphasis on skill with bow and lance... Youths from the old military families of the northwest trained in weapons from an early age, and the imperial family was no exception... The T'ang ideal was *ju-hsiang, ch'u chiang* – a man who was equally accomplished at court or on campaign."[22]

The emphasis on skill for elite troops (often contrasted with the rather more basic abilities of the rank and file) continued during the Song Dynasty, with martial skills based examinations and creation of elite units of "picked men," the equivalent of modern special forces.[23]

Attention was paid to unarmed combat as well, where the new kung fu styles being developed were put to the test through regular competitions:

"Soldiers of the *chin-chun*, or palace guard, were trained in unarmed combat, and held regular boxing matches between units to maintain standards."[24]

As such, we can say that the period of the Tang and Northern Song dynasties was when kung fu really came into its own, experiencing a golden age at the same time as Chinese culture as a whole.

Kung fu needed this prolonged period of stability married to cultural development and a rise in popular entertainment to achieve a new level of sophistication.

This is not to say there was any lack of violence and war to hone its effectiveness, but this was not the kind of total war of the Warring States that would have left neither space nor time to develop the individuality of one's skills.

That is why styles, weapons and fighting methods created during this period do not look too dissimilar to the ones still practised today, which earlier periods such as the Han and the Warring States cannot claim.

Chapter 7

Invasion and the Rise of the South

This chapter deals with a period of crisis in China, when the country was repeatedly invaded by foreign armies but, at the same time, when the south of China was fully colonised and when southern kung fu styles came into being.

Despite its promising start, the Song Dynasty was never as strong as the Tang militarily. Almost from the start, Song China was under threat from foreign states on its northern and western borders and in the year 1127, the Jin, a race related to the Manchus, attacked and captured the north of China, including the capital, Changang. They even took hostage both the reigning emperor, Qingzong, and his father Emperor Huizong, who had abdicated in favour of his son in the vain hope of preventing the brewing crisis.

The Move Away from the Northern Heartlands

The Song Dynasty regrouped and moved its capital south of the Yangtze River to Nanjing, with Qingzong's younger brother ascending to the throne as Emperor Gaozong. However, the nature of the

Chinese civilisation would be greatly altered, setting in motion a shift in the centre of gravity from the north to the south.

Before this time, the south was never fully civilised, even though it was technically within the borders of the Empire from the Han Dynasty onwards. Its peoples were considered very definitely not Chinese, but uncivilised and dangerous barbarians. Lewis summarises the view of the South held by most Chinese, until the Southern Song Dynasty:

"In literature ranging over a millennium, from the Han through the Tang periods, the south is described as a region of swamps and jungles, diseases and poisonous plants, savage animals and even more savage tattooed tribesmen."[1]

Many an aristocrat who lost the favour of the emperor was sent to be the governor or some other official in Guangdong or Fujian. Such a posting was considered to be little better than exile.

Now, however, with their ancestral plains of the Yellow River no longer within reach, the Chinese began to truly colonise the mountains, forests and the long coastline of the south, creating new cities and opening up new ports for trade.

China had no choice but to reinvent itself, and it opened up to the outside world, increasing maritime trade a hundredfold.

Although the Southern Song never could match the power of the Northern Song, let alone the Tang and Han Empires, it was soon wealthier than any of them, thanks to this new interest in commerce.[2]

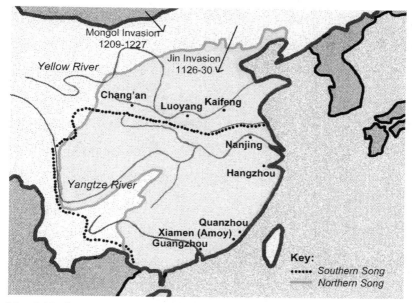

Map 4: Northern and Southern Song Dynasty

The Story of Yue Fei

In cultural terms, the Southern Song saw a retreat to conservatism, with the neo-Confucianism promulgated by the 12th-century philosopher Zhu Xi in ascendancy over both Buddhism and Daoism.

The same conservatism and caution also pervaded political discourse. The imperial court was at first split between generals who wanted to attack the Jin invaders and win back the north and those who wanted a truce and the security of peace.

This set the scene for one of the most famous incidents in Chinese history, the story of Marshal Yue Fei (1103–1142).

Yue Fei was born into a dark time for China, in the years leading up to the Jin invasion. His mother taught him from a very young age that it was his filial duty to serve his country and she was said to have tattooed the words "Save the State" on young Yue Fei's back as a constant reminder of his obligation.

Her son duly joined the army and rose very quickly through the ranks due to his prodigious martial skills – he was said to be an incomparable archer and spear fighter – and attained the high rank of marshal at a very young age.

So successful were his campaigns against the Jin in the north that he pushed back the Jin armies and found himself within striking range of the Jin capital itself.

It was at this crucial moment that he was recalled from the front in the north by imperial decree, being forced to turn back on the eve of what could have been a famous victory and a chance to once again reunify the country.

The reason for this strange decision by the Emperor was that the anti-war faction at the Song court did not believe that the territory Yue Fei had already re-conquered could be secured and held in the long term and they were scared of the likely retribution by the Jin.

Upon his return, Marshal Yue Fei was arrested on trumped-up charges of treason and hastily executed. However, popular outcry at his death was such that the Song Emperor quickly diverted responsibility and blame for the decision onto Prime Minister Qin Hui, one of the leaders of the anti-war faction, and had him executed in turn along with his whole family.

To this day, Chinese people everywhere curse the Prime Minister's name. His family surname has been erased from all records and is no longer in use, and visitors to his tomb in Hangzhou still spit at it in memory of his betrayal of a Chinese national hero.

As a final act of retribution, the fried twisted sticks of dough Chinese people eat for breakfast are said to represent the Prime Minister and his wife being tortured for eternity by continually being submerged in boiling oil.

To understand this no doubt one of the most spectacular and sustained acts of retribution against an individual by a whole nation, you have to understand the psychological scars left on the Chinese historical memory by the trauma of successive invasions and defeats suffered by the Empire, of which the loss of the north to the Jin was but the first step.

To China, Yue Fei represented a memory of past greatness of the Han, the Tang and the Northern Song and a last opportunity to regain that greatness – if only history were reversed and Marshal Yue Fei was allowed to complete his war and reunify China.

Whether or not he would have been successful, had he not been re-called, is something we will never know. It may well have turned out that the anti-war party led by Qin Hui would have been proved right and, overextended by its military adventures, Song China would have collapsed sooner, instead of surviving for another century after Yue Fei's death. That, however, is beside the point, for Yue Fei was and remains important to the Chinese as a symbol of national pride, strength, honour and loyalty, rather than for any actual achievements in war.

The Mongol Invasion and Ming Reconquest

After Marshal Yue Fei's aborted attempt to reconquer the north, the Song Dynasty continued, but the trajectory of Chinese history was now set inexorably downwards from the high point of the Tang, at least in military terms.

When a new power, the Mongols, appeared in the north, the Song court decided to ally with them against the Jin in what proved to be a very costly mistake. The unstoppable Mongol horde quickly overwhelmed the Jin Empire, but they did not stop there. They went on to attack the Song themselves, pushing their armies into the sea in Guangdong.

A new Mongol dynasty, the Yuan, extinguished the Song in the year 1279 and so, for the first time in Chinese history, the Empire was entirely under the rule of its foreign conquerors.

At first, the Mongols had little interest in adopting Chinese culture and tried to maintain their separate identity by living apart from their subjects in huge yurt settlements, and maintaining their own language and dress.

However, over time, there was an increasing conflict between Mongol conservatives and a new generation who wanted to enjoy the trappings of civilisation offered by the Chinese. Over the following ninety years, the balance of power between the two groups shifted back and forth and, in the end, the very existence of this unresolved conflict at the heart of the Yuan Dynasty made it vulnerable to a reversal.

In 1368, eighty-nine years after the final collapse of the Song, the Yuan Dynasty itself collapsed and China was reconquered by the Chinese warlord Zhu Yuanzhang (1328–1398), who went on to establish the Ming Dynasty.

The Ming were rich and powerful and a fully Chinese dynasty, with countless cultural achievements, such as the mass introduction of printing which led to the popularisation of literature and the writing of China's greatest novels, *The Romance of the Three Kingdoms*, *Journey to the West*, and *The Water Margin* (also known as *The Outlaws of the Marsh*).

This was also the time when the Three Jewel Eunuch, the Admiral Zheng He (1371–1433), made his famous voyages of discovery into the Indian Ocean, beating the great journeys of Da Gama and Columbus by almost a century.[3]

Nonetheless, there was a pervasive sense of unease in the political sphere. Scarred by the defeats by the Jin and the Mongols, the Ming emperors felt insecure on the throne and never had the confidence, the unerring conviction and the sense of their own supreme power enjoyed by the Han or the Tang emperors before them.

Instead, the Ming Empire was a place of secret police and informants and frequent purges of officials by a suspicious state.

Suspicion tends to be self-fulfilling and so the Ming suffered from regular rebellions by various factions unhappy with the central government. In the end, it was indeed an internal rebellion that ended the dynasty so ignobly, with the last Emperor committing suicide by hanging himself from the bough of a locust tree behind the Forbidden City in Beijing.[4]

The Ming's powerful northern neighbour, the Kingdom of the Manchu, took advantage of the chaos and invaded, so launching the last dynasty, the Qing, in 1644.

The Southern School of Kung Fu

The previous flowering of different styles and schools of kung fu in the Northern Song continued and accelerated after the dynasty moved south. In fact, Lorge follows Lin Boyuan in believing that the creation of the very concept that there could be different schools of kung fu with their lineages and special techniques took place during the Southern Song.[5]

The opening up of southern China by the Southern Song Dynasty also led directly to the rise of the Nan Quan or Southern Fist family of kung fu styles.

Fujian Province, which grew rapidly thanks to the opening up of major ports in Fuzhou, Quanzhou and Amoy (also known as Xiamen) in preceding centuries, saw much growth and diversity of kung fu styles in the Song and Ming dynasties, including a number of styles that mimicked animal movements such as Tiger, Dragon, Monkey and Buffalo.

The style I practise, White Crane, or Bai He Quan, was created right at the end of the Ming Dynasty in the first half of the 17th century by Lady Fang Qi Niang. She combined the principles of evasive movements and pressure point strikes she developed by watching the movements of a crane, with the foundation of Southern Shaolin kung fu taught to her by her father.

Known as the Scholars' Style in later years, Bai He Quan would become one of the most important styles of southern kung fu, spreading throughout Fujian and neighbouring provinces from its base in the village of Yongchun and influencing, among other styles, both Wing Chun and the styles of Okinawan karate.

Meanwhile, in northern China, there was continuous development in Long Arm boxing – Chang Quan – family of styles, the oldest of which was Taizu, which, according to tradition, was created by the first emperor of the Song Dynasty, Song Taizu, who gave it his own name.

Many of the northern styles practised today, including Baji Quan, Pigua Quan, Liu He Quan and Cha Quan have connections both with Chang Quan and with Muslim Heritage martial arts, thanks to the opening up of links with the Muslim world during the Yuan Dynasty.[6]

Weapons and Changes in the Army

The period of the Song and Ming dynasties was when many of the traditional Chinese weapons still used in kung fu practice today were first created or were perfected, thanks to a rich mixture of traditional Chinese, Jin and Mongol influences, leaving a truly impressive variety of swords, broadswords, spears, cudgels, tridents and halberds being used.[7]

Marshal Yue Fei himself was a great spear fighter, as has been mentioned, and he is said to have invented the shape of the hook spear by adding a downward-curving hook jutting out at ninety degrees to the main blade of the spear, which could be used to hit an opponent on a reverse thrust, as well as to unseat a horseman.[8]

Chinese armies of the Ming Dynasty continued where the Song left off, relying on infantry and cavalry armed with bows, lances, spears, halberds and swords. But there were two key changes: first, guns and other projectile weapons powered by gunpowder gained an important role in the arsenal during the Ming, whereas they were still only on the periphery of Song Armies.[9]

Second, the status of the military officer class declined in China in the Southern Song and Ming, when compared to the high esteem in which the warrior was held by the Han, Tang and the first few reigns of Northern Song. This is related to the fact that during the Song, the long running process of separation of the literati elite from the class of military families was made complete. The literati were now a professional scholarly class, selected by examination, while the influence of the old aristocratic families, with their culture of military service, was much reduced.[10]

Peers has the following to say about the situation in the Ming Dynasty:

"After the Yung Lo period the emperors tended to live very sheltered lives at court, and so were not able or inclined to supervise the army personally; military affairs were left to the bureaucrats of the Board of War, who regarded the generals as their social inferiors and often suspected the able ones of disloyalty. The last emperor to take the field himself was Hsuan-te, who in 1428 personally killed several Mongols."[11]

This loss of prestige by the martial arts at the highest levels of Chinese society fitted into the pattern of a general lack of confidence in political life caused by the successive defeats of previous centuries.

Despite this general trend, the Ming Dynasty saw a number of significant martial arts theorists emerge from both the military elites and the literati. These included General Yu Dayou (1503–1579), of whom more later, and General Qi Jiguang (1528–1588), who wrote the first kung fu manual, the *New Manual on Military Efficiency*, which mentioned free-hand fighting and listed as many as sixteen different styles of kung fu.

From the literati we have such famous names as Wu Shu (1611–1695), who spent decades travelling across China to learn different spear fighting styles and published a compilation of them called simply *Arm Exercises*, and Cheng Zongyou, who, after having spent

10 years studying at the Shaolin Monastery, wrote the earliest text (compiled c. 1610) describing the Shaolin staff method, titled *Exposition of the Original Shaolin Staff Method*.[12]

The Flowering of Shaolin Kung Fu

From Ming Dynasty sources, we finally have the first verifiable evidence of Shaolin kung fu being practised at the Shaolin Monastery.[13] A number of martial arts techniques and styles were developed there, including the classic Luohan Fist freehand forms and the staff fighting for which Shaolin is famous.

In addition to developing its own styles of kung fu, the Shaolin Monastery used its fame to become a key training centre for other martial artists, often inviting famous masters from other styles to visit and teach in the Monastery in order to exchange knowledge and skills. In this way, Shaolin acted much like a leading university of today, akin to Oxford or Harvard, becoming a centre of excellence and drawing in talent from across the Empire.

An example of this is the story of General Yu Dayou from Fujian Province, who was an expert martial artist himself, and, upon hearing stories of the skill Shaolin monks had with the staff, travelled to the Monastery to see for himself in the year 1560. Left unimpressed, he then proceeded to teach the monks his own variant of the staff method, which he recorded in his *Sword Classic (Jian Jing)*.[14]

The scholar Tang Hao later argued that the Five Tigers Interception staff method General Yu taught to the monks was still practised by them in parallel to their own staff patterns.[15]

This example explains why so many disparate styles today claim a lineage back to the Shaolin Monastery. In some cases, these styles were developed by the Shaolin warrior monks themselves; in other cases, they were developed independently by masters who spent only a limited time at the Monastery, exchanging knowledge.

The fame of the Shaolin Monastery and its kung fu really spread across China thanks to its monks' involvement in the suppression of Japanese wokou pirates, who plagued Zhejiang, Fujian and the whole southeast coast at the time.

In 1553, the Emperor was forced to send his army south to defend the coastline from these attacks, and a unit of Buddhist warrior monks from a number of monasteries including Shaolin and under the leadership of Shaolin monk Tianyuan, were included among the troops.[16]

After the successful campaign, the monks were celebrated as heroes and their kung fu skills entered public consciousness, so much so, that Shaolin fighting and Shaolin staff entered popular idiom as examples of martial prowess.[17]

It is possible that it was at the end of this campaign in the southeast that the South Shaolin Monastery in Fujian Province was first established. Certainly legends in Fujian Province connect the establishment of the Monastery with Shaolin monks repelling attacks by pirates, though many of the legends claim this happened during the Tang Dynasty and not the Ming.

Since few records of the South Shaolin Monastery can be verifiably traced, it is impossible to be sure. Shahar, in his investigation of Shaolin history, has found no mention of an earlier Tang Dynasty campaign against Japanese pirates.

Although the fighting that the historical Ming Dynasty unit of monks engaged in happened in Zhejiang and not Fujian, the two provinces are next to each other, so some monks staying behind to establish another outpost of the main Henan Shaolin Monastery is not outside the bounds of possibility. One thing that is certain is that South Shaolin would play a key role in the history of kung fu as a symbol of resistance to the Qing, so it must have been established at some point before the end of the Ming Dynasty.

Internal Cultivation

The Southern Song, Yuan and Ming period continued to see the importance of cultivation practices, both as part of kung fu practice and in society as a whole.

After the conquest of China by the Mongols and then on and off during the Ming and the Qing dynasties, the idea of personal perfection via internal alchemy, qi gong and meditation was sometimes frowned upon by the state on the basis of it being a "selfish" practice and also, unspoken, because the idea of individual empowerment inherent in personal practice was a challenge to central authority.[18]

It did little to stem its popularity, with the Ming Dynasty in particular seeing endless Daoist and Buddhist-inspired cults being established, often combining some forms of kung fu and nei gong practice. Even the first Emperor of the Ming started his path to the throne as a member and then a leader of one such Buddhist cult, the Red Turbans.[19]

Some measure of how established nei gong was can be glimpsed from the fact that even the third of the three great traditions of China, and arguably the least metaphysical of them, Confucianism, also began to develop in the direction of internal cultivation by the Song Dynasty, perhaps in response to its two rivals, Buddhism and Daoism. This blending of nei gong and Confucianism produced the idea of physically experiencing a state of perfection and clarity, as espoused by the philosopher Wang Yang Ming (1472–1529).

As we have seen already, the Ming Dynasty also saw a number of key texts connecting internal cultivation and kung fu practice written down for the first time, including the *Yi Jin Jing* in 1624, and the work on the Wudang "internal school" by Huang Zhongxi (1610–1695) and his son Huang Baijia (1643–?).

However, the greatest surge in internal cultivation within kung fu practice would happen during the next dynasty, the Qing.

Chapter 8

Kung Fu as Resistance

This chapter looks at the end of the Chinese Imperial Period, when, under threat from the Manchus, Chinese people turned to kung fu as a means to fight the invaders and hold onto their identity, in the process making kung fu what it is today.

The Manchus who conquered China in 1644 learned the lessons from the failure of the Yuan Dynasty. From the start, they both integrated themselves much more deeply into the bureaucracy and structures of the Chinese state, fully accepting the fruits of Chinese civilisation, and at the same time kept themselves racially distinct from the conquered population.

Policy of Subjugation

The Manchus went about establishing their domination, however, in the most appalling manner:

> "The Manchus had treated the Chinese as a subject race. They had expelled all Chinese from Manchuria and confiscated large areas of land inside China, treating the peasants as slaves. Manchus and Chinese were segregated, intermarriage was banned and while footbinding was forbidden for

Manchus, the Chinese men were forced to shave their hair in front and wear the hated Manchu queue (plait). In Beijing, Chinese were expelled from the northern city (the Forbidden City and official dwellings) and forced to live in the 'Chinese city' in the south."[1]

The hair-cutting "queue" edict of 1645 triggered fierce resistance among the Chinese population, who saw it as a visible symbol of their subjugation. There were many rebellions across China, but they were eventually put down with overwhelming force.

One result of these rebellions and the later Wars of Three Feudatories, when the Manchu court had to put down rebellions by three Han Chinese warlords who held lands in the south of China, was further edicts forbidding the Chinese civilian population from openly carrying certain types of weapons and in particular firearms, the use of which was becoming more and more widespread by this time.[2]

Open practice of martial arts by the Han Chinese civilians also met with disapproval, as such practitioners were often bunched together with rebels and troublemakers in the eyes of local officials and were therefore harassed and persecuted.

Such harsh measures ensured continuing dogged resistance to Manchu rule. The Chinese fought back against the Manchus in a way they did not against the Mongols, the Jin or the Toba Wei before them, perhaps seeing a greater existential threat from these new conquerors, who did not just keep themselves to themselves but actively wanted to appropriate China.

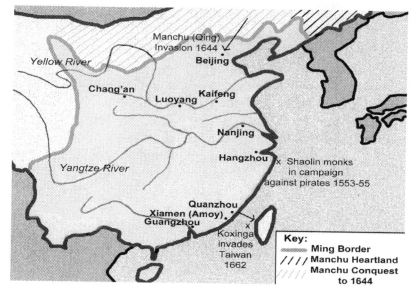

Map 5: Ming Dynasty and Qing Conquest

Koxinga and Military Resistance

Open military resistance to the Manchus lasted from the 1640s to the 1660s as Chinese armies coalesced around the surviving princes of the Ming Royal House and fought a defensive war, gradually being pushed back into the southeast and southwest corners of China – Fujian and Yunnan provinces respectively – both of which had strong natural defences in their mountainous landscapes.

However, the Manchu troops gradually tightened the noose and hunted down the royal princes of the Ming one by one. By 1660, the only notable rebel still fighting was General Zheng Chenggong (1624–1662), otherwise known as Koxinga, who had a powerbase on the Fujianese coast and a fleet of his own, which allowed him to command the sea between Fujian and Taiwan.

Koxinga was able to inflict some serious reverses on the Manchus over a decade of fighting, but by the early 1660s, it was clear that the Ming cause was lost.

In 1662, Koxinga instead took his fleet across the Taiwan Strait and, in a surprise attack, took over Taiwan from its Dutch colonial occupiers. Ensconced on the island, Koxinga's son was able to hold the Qing at bay for another twenty years, until 1683. When Taiwan finally fell, it was the last piece of the Chinese Empire to come under Qing rule.

The failure of open resistance to Qing rule by the princes and generals of the Ming did not, however, mean the end of all resistance. Many former officers of the Ming army abandoned their posts and dissolved into the general populace, particularly on the south coast in Fujian and Guangdong.

There, these rebels formed secret societies such as the Hong Men (Red Gate) Society, with a shared objective of bringing down the Qing and restoring the Ming. These societies carried out terrorist activities against the Qing state throughout the 18th and into the 19th centuries, by which time many of them had turned into criminal syndicates, the precursors of the modern-day triads.

In the meantime, the Qing Dynasty was politically successful in its first hundred and fifty years, under the rule of three strong emperors: Kangxi (1654–1722), Yongzheng (1678–1735) and Qianlong (1711–1799).

Kangxi and Qianlong in particular are remembered by history as great scholars in their own right and even more importantly as patrons of scholarship, commissioning great encyclopaedias that summarised the collective wisdom and art of preceding centuries.

During these three reigns, the Qing were able to push the borders of China much further than they had ever been, even when compared to the high points of Han and Tang rule. Under Kangxi, vast swathes of Mongolia, southern Siberia around lake Baikal, and Tibet were all added to the Empire. Under Qianlong, the area of China reached its maximum extent of 11.5 million square kilometres, with the further addition of territory in Central Asia, while the population topped 163 million.[3]

Wars and Rebellions

Like all dynasties before them, the Qing also started to weaken towards the end, producing a string of rulers who were not up to the challenge of the times. In the 19th century, China went through a period of great social upheaval. China's territory and sovereignty were increasingly encroached upon by Western powers, Britain foremost among them. To redress the trade imbalance with China, British agents spread the use of opium among the Chinese populace and, in so doing, created an artificial demand in the drug that allowed them to establish a monopoly in the opium trade.

Seeing the corrupting effects of opium addiction, the Qing government belatedly banned its use, which precipitated the Opium Wars with Britain and other Western powers in 1839–42 and again in 1856–60.

The Manchus could not match Western firepower and were defeated and forced to cede territory, including Hong Kong Island, and trade concessions to the West.

For the first time, China was forced to face up to the fact that it was no longer the most powerful and technologically advanced nation on Earth, a role it had laid claim to (whether or not it was always accurate) since the Han Dynasty, both under indigenous Chinese rule and when ruled by the Mongols and the Manchus.

In addition to the humiliation Qing China suffered in these wars, it was also hit by major rebellions. The biggest by far was the Taiping Rebellion in the middle of the 19th century, when as many as 20 million Chinese citizens died in the name of a religious cult only distantly inspired by Christianity, which was led by Hong Xiuchuan (1814–1864).

For over a decade, between 1850 and 1864, Hong's followers were able to establish their own independent quasi-religious state south of the Yangtze River, with their capital in Nanjing, before the Qing finally managed to suppress them.[4]

Smaller than the Taiping Rebellion but more famous – or perhaps notorious is the more accurate word – was the Boxer Rebellion in 1898. It was so called because of the significant number of martial arts practitioners who took part. In reality, most of these were peasants with a limited amount of martial training, who were duped by cult leaders that the qi gong exercises they practised as part of their kung fu training would protect them from all harm, including bullets.[5]

Thousands ended up being killed by the Qing and by Western troops, who were helping the Manchu state and were armed with the latest guns. It was a sorry incident that demonstrated the darker side of the cults and secret societies that sprang up initially to oppose the Qing, but then turned to crime and superstition.

Having said this, not all the Boxer rebels were duped. Among them were plenty of brave souls who must have understood the futility of going up against guns, but could not let go of even the smallest chance of ridding their country both of the old Manchu invaders and the newer Western colonialists in one go.

The penultimate emperor of the Qing Dynasty, Guangxu (1875–1908), did attempt to reform his vast country in order to be better able to compete with the West and try to channel popular anger and frustration into something more constructive. However, he did not have sufficient support for his progressive policies and, in a coup reminiscent of the rise of Wu Zetian during the Tang Dynasty, Guangxu's aunt, the Empress Dowager Cixi (1835–1908), took over the reins of power and made him a virtual prisoner within his own palace in the Forbidden City. Unlike Wu Zetian, Cixi did not take the final step of proclaiming herself Emperor, but nonetheless ruled like one in all but name until her death in 1908.

Cixi's death left her great-nephew, the 3-year-old Puyi (1906–1967), on the Throne of Heaven, for Guangxu himself died in mysterious circumstances just a day before his aunt.[6]

Unsurprisingly, the boy Emperor was not in a position to face the unprecedented challenges of the 20th century that would have taxed a Han Wudi or Tang Taizong at the height of their powers.

The country quickly fell under the control of rival warlords and, in

1912, Puyi abdicated the throne, bringing the Chinese imperial line, which had lasted from the times of the Xia, to an abrupt and ignoble end.

Kung Fu under the Qing

The majority of kung fu styles practised today date from the Qing Dynasty. This is partly due to the natural life cycle in the practice of any traditional art form, as old styles die out or merge with others to create new ones, with few surviving the test of time. However, it is also due to the unique conditions in the 17th, 18th and 19th centuries, with a potent mixture of invasion, rebellions and the encroachment of modernity.

The persecution of Ming rebels and the prohibitions against open practice of martial arts enacted by the Qing led to martial arts being practised in secret behind closed doors. For this reason, each style was practised by a smaller circle of people (sometimes by members of a single family – hence the so-called family styles such as Hung Gar or Lau Gar), often with little contact or exchange of skills with other styles for extended periods of time.

These conditions would have made it more difficult for large systems such as Shaolin, Wudang or Bai He Quan to develop, taking in many different sub-styles into their fold. Instead, as masters worked to develop new skills in near isolation from each other, skills and techniques were not mixed together into a bigger system, but rather each new development was more likely to end up being a separate style. This encouraged a greater number and variety of styles, but with each one having a much smaller number of practitioners.

The second reason for the variety is that the sheer violence of the Qing society, particularly in its later period, acted like a pressure cooker for martial arts. The greater demand for effective ways to protect oneself in an age of wars, rebellions and secret societies increased competition between styles and acted as a kind of natural selection of quality.

New styles were tested as never before and those that did not provide their practitioners with the ability to survive were quickly replaced by more effective styles.

This is one reason why styles from this period tend to be less elaborate, with shorter patterns, which were easier and quicker to learn, and with an emphasis on power and hard conditioning to maximise their destructive force, sometimes even at the expense of the long-term health of the practitioner.

Southern Styles and the Burning of South Shaolin

Because the southeast corner of China in Fujian and Guangdong was the area that resisted the Qing the longest, as we have seen, and also was the area where their control was weakest, it is not surprising that a disproportionate number of kung fu styles that were created in the Qing Dynasty originated from these two provinces, including such well known styles as Wuzhu, Hung Gar, Wing Chun, Mei Hua and Choy Li Fut.

Many of these styles were connected in one way or another with the South Shaolin Monastery in Fujian, which, according to tradition, was burned down by the Qing troops in retribution for acting as a centre of resistance to Manchu rule, either in the year 1674 or 1732, according to rival traditions.

It is hard to distinguish between fact and fiction where the South Monastery is concerned, but it is certainly true that the Monastery ceased to exist during the Qing Dynasty and was destroyed so completely that even any mentions in official records have been expunged – a common practice during the Qing Dynasty against organisations or individuals who challenged the Manchu. In recent years rival excavations and research in three sites in Fujian – Putian, Quanzhou and Fuqing – have all claimed to have found the "real" temple, with some evidence, like temple foundations, pottery, and mill stones bearing the glyphs "Shaolin" having been uncovered.[7]

According to legend, the five monks who survived the burning of the Monastery became the five ancestors who spread the skills of Shaolin among the general populace. The Wuzhu or Five Ancestor Fist style is said to have been created based on their teachings.

Shahar mentions that this legend was incorporated into the foundation myth of the Heaven and Earth Society (Tiandihui), better known in the West as the Triads, and that the legends originate mostly in the South of China where the Shaolin name may have become associated with local Buddhist temples:

"The motif of the Shaolin Monastery's burning is likely related to Fujian lore concerning the conflagration of a local southern Shaolin Temple, and the name Changlin, which is mentioned in several versions, has been shown to designate a historical monastery in that province. Some scholars consider it the source of the brotherhood's foundation myth."[8]

My own research and interviews with representatives of all three claimants to South Shaolin name – i.e. Putian, Fuqing and Quanzhou temples[9] – leads me to believe that there *was* a physical temple in Fujian, and maybe even more than one, where martial arts were practised and which therefore may have become a centre for underground societies during the Qing Dynasty. As a Buddhist Monastery with practising kung fu monks it may have been referred to locally as "Shaolin" purely because by that time the name Shaolin became a kind of short-hand for any temples and monasteries associated with kung fu, or it may have had some loose association with the main Henan Shaolin Monastery in the manner of subsidiary shrine (fangtou), which Shahar and Lorge both mention as a possible way in which loosely affiliated monks may have coexisted with the main Shaolin Monastery.[10]

In fact, Shahar notes research by Wen Yucheng and Zhou Weliang, which showed that a "Shaolin Cloister" (Shaolin yuan) existed in Fuqing, one of the possible locations of the South Shaolin Monastery since the Southern Song period, though "neither its relation to the Henan Temple nor its military history are clear".[11]

More research in this area is required to be more sure.

Kung Fu and Nei Dan

This tradition of kung fu masters escaping and teaching the general population illustrates a more general fact that the large number of ex-Ming Dynasty officers and soldiers who left the army during the Qing Dynasty's takeover brought the teaching of kung fu to the peasant communities wherever they settled down.

The sudden access of peasants to the art of kung fu dramatically increased the number of people able to practise it. It also changed the nature of kung fu itself, for example by injecting into it a whole new arsenal of weapons based on farming tools and implements, such as the section staffs, the hoe, the stool and various types of knives. This was helped by the Qing prohibition on the carrying of military weapons, which made it necessary to find alternatives to swords and firearms.

This popularisation of what used to be a relatively exclusive practice of kung fu was paralleled by a similar popularisation of internal alchemy practice, or nei dan, a direct descendant of internal cultivation techniques of earlier years.

According to Kirkland, literati Daoists during the Qing dynasty simplified the tenets of internal alchemy to make it "more accessible, and more attractive, to the public by removing more and more of the esoteric symbolism that had characterized medieval nei-tan texts... [these more accessible texts] also eventuated in various appropriations by non-Taoists. For instance, Taoist inspiration was claimed by many twentieth-century martial-arts teachers..."[12]

This process of popularisation was no doubt helped both by greater availability of literature through printing from the Ming onwards, and the wholesale disruption of barriers between different social orders by the trauma of the Manchu invasion, and the ensuing resistance to it at all levels of society. For example, Kirkland also mentions that more literati during the Qing associated themselves with Daoism – as opposed to the Lamaist Buddhism of the Manchu – as an act of cultural defiance.[13]

Both kung fu and nei dan were often perceived as part of the same "secret" teaching by the population at large. If anything, the physical aspects of such Buddhist and Daoist practices made them more accessible to the lower orders through the meeting of quite practical objectives of treating ailments, learning to fight and conducting religious ceremonies for the community. It introduced the population to philosophical concepts of the Three Traditions that may otherwise have remained esoteric and inaccessible by anyone but the highly educated elite.

However, there was also a more negative consequence of this popularisation of kung fu and nei dan. Printing may have broadened the access to philosophy among the middle classes, but the peasantry was still illiterate in most cases.

That, combined with the violence of society at large, meant that, in many cases, the ancient connections between kung fu and the philosophical traditions of China that informed key aspects of it, for example internal cultivation of energy, were misrepresented and wilfully perverted by leaders of popular cults such as the White Lotus in southern China.

This unfortunately made something like the Boxer Rebellion more likely, as the martial artists involved would have been less able to distinguish truth from fiction in the claims of magical power and invulnerability made by cult leaders, who goaded them on to attack the guns of the Manchus and their Western backers.

The combination of kung fu and internal cultivation practices during the Qing Dynasty had a more fortuitous consequence in the flowering of internal styles of kung fu such as Tai Ji Quan, Bagua, and Xing Yi. They developed from the internal principles of older styles, including Wudang Quan, as well as the nei gong and qi gong practices popular among scholars and gentry at this time.

For once there are plenty of written sources surviving, which detail how these styles were created in the period starting in late Ming, through the Ming/Qing transition and during the Qing Dynasty itself. These include, to name but three key examples: the aforementioned *Yi Jin Jing*, dating from 1624; Huang Baijia's (1643 – ?) account of Wang Zhengnan's internal kung fu called *Art of the Internal School*; and the *Neigong Tushuo* treatise published in 1882 by Wang Zuyuan (ca. 1820 – after 1882).

Such is the wealth of sources from this period that scholars like Lorge and Shahar argue that the Qing Dynasty and the late Ming was the time when the connection between kung fu and internal cultivation practices, including the Daoist gymnastics of daoyin, was first forged. In this they are following the example of Lin Boyuan, who was the first to suggest this timing.[14]

I have already presented by case against this theory, arguing that the far greater number of sources is simply due to the explosion of printing, and so of literature of every kind, during the Ming and Qing. The far fewer and less direct sources form the Warring States and Han Dynasty periods, nonetheless, to my mind, show that what happened during the Qing Dynasty was a culmination of a long process of development rather than its creation.

However, it is impossible not to acknowledge that the whole process of synthesis between kung fu and daoyin and nei gong seems to have accelerated, or, perhaps, it is better to say that it reached a new height, during the late Ming and the Qing.

Shahar explains it well by demonstrating how kung fu treatises from the Qing period are full of references to "internal strength" (nei li), "qi cultivation" (lian qi), and "circulating qi" (yun qi).[15] And the synthesis goes further than just the concept of qi, to include other ideas of Chinese philosophy and cosmology:

"Beginning in the late Ming, many authors were no longer

satisfied to describe limb movements only. Instead, they embedded fighting postures in the rich vocabularies of medicine, religion, and philosophy. Martial artists identified within their own bodies the universal forces of *yin* and *yang*, the five elements, and eight trigrams, investing the martial arts with a cosmological dimension."[16]

All of these ideas have been linked to martial arts practice before, as we have seen in preceding chapters and in the quotations given from far older classics, but during the Qing Dynasty a whole new symbolic language for the martial arts can be said to have been developed, one that is in use to this day.

The Karate Connection

One last key development in martial arts over this period that should be mentioned is the connection between kung fu and karate.

To fully explain the links between karate and kung fu would require a book of its own. Suffice to say here that the parallels between the two martial arts traditions are very extensive and are the result of the influence of Chinese civilisation both on Okinawa, where karate was invented, and Japan, where it was further developed.

A number of Okinawan masters are known to have travelled to Fujian Province during the 19th century, training in kung fu schools in Fuzhou City. This included the celebrated school run by Master Xie Zhongxiang of Ming He Quan, or Calling Crane kung fu, who to this day is remembered by his nickname Ryuru Ko in both China and Japan.[17]

This exchange allowed for the principles of Crane style, as well as Tiger and other Fujianese styles, to be injected into indigenous Okinawan martial arts, influencing among others: Kanryo Higaonna's Shorei Ryu, Chojun Miyagi's Goju Ryu, Kanbun Uechi's Uechi Ryu, and Norisato Nakaima's Ryuei Ryu styles of karate.[18]

The Qing Dynasty was also when the famous Bible of Karate, the *Bubishi* (*Wu Bei Zhi* in Chinese), a classic of Chinese kung fu, was transmitted to Okinawa, explaining the principles of Crane styles of kung fu and greatly influencing Okinawan and Japanese martial arts.[19]

I mentioned in the Introduction that karate has borrowed from kung fu the key essence of the internal cultivation practices of qi, a fact the *Bubishi* confirms. To this can also be added the borrowing of principles of traditional Chinese medicine, Chinese philosophy and a range of weapons that were first created in China and then made their way across the sea to Okinawa and Japan.

As such, karate and kung fu should rightly be seen as sister martial arts traditions sharing much of their heritage. This means that the philosophy and history of kung fu discussed in this book are of importance for a fuller understanding of karate just as much as for kung fu itself.

Part 3

Philosophy of Kung Fu

Chapter 9

The Shared Heritage of Chinese Culture

This chapter sets out some of the key concepts in Chinese culture, including the Dao, Yin and Yang, the Five Elements and the Eight Trigrams, and considers what they mean for the martial arts.

Having set out the origins and the historical development of kung fu, I hope I have been able to demonstrate how closely linked kung fu practice has been to the wider Chinese culture down through the centuries, changing to reflect the key events of each epoch in Chinese history.

It should be clear that kung fu is much more than just a set of fighting methods, but a whole philosophy and culture in its own right.

Correlative Reasoning

The first thing you notice about Chinese culture is the remarkable extent to which everything in China is interconnected. Concepts and principles are shared across schools of philosophy, artistic disciplines and even religions, with no apparent tension or contradiction. This is what people refer to as the holistic nature of Chinese civilisation.

In the Chinese world-view, everything under Heaven is governed by the natural movements of the Way – the Dao – and everything is a product of the interplay between the two powers, Yin and Yang, the succession of the Five Elements, Wu Xing, and the patterns of the eight trigrams, the Ba Gua.

These same principles govern disciplines that, on the surface, seem to have little to do with each other, such as calligraphy and cooking, poetry and gardening, and of course kung fu itself.

So, when a cook prepares a dish, he has to be careful about balancing the flavours in a way that is based on the balance of Yin and Yang and the Five Elements. Likewise, when a gardener creates a garden, he will integrate a water feature and trees and shrubs, striving for balance and a spontaneous naturalness and quietude, recalling the characteristics said to be inherent of the Dao.

Angus Graham, in his seminal work *Disputers of the Tao*, explained this as a product of a correlative system of reasoning; that is to say an archaic world-view common to all ancient societies, which connects objects and events together into a larger pattern to explain the world and man's place in it. In the case of the West, that world-view was gradually displaced by the causal view of the world characteristic of science.[1]

In China, that transition never took place in quite the same clear-cut way, despite China's own many scientific discoveries. In fact, even in the modern world of globalisation and universality of science, the Chinese culture still retains its parallel holistic approach. Traditional Chinese acupuncture, for example, is fully worked out on the principles of Yin and Yang and qi cosmology, and yet is used alongside "Western" medicine in Chinese hospitals (and increasingly in hospitals in the West as well), because it has a proven efficacy from the causal "scientific" viewpoint as well as from the traditional correlative viewpoint.

The Three Religions

The three great religions of China – Confucianism, Daoism and Buddhism – have been carefully woven into this correlative system. These religions coexist in China, occupying their respective places in the pattern of Chinese civilisation with far less friction than, for example, between Islam, Judaism and Christianity in the West.

This is evidenced by the oft-remarked upon fact that the average Chinese man or woman will likely integrate elements of all three religions, as well as local folk beliefs, into their day-to-day religious practice, observing Confucian filial piety with respect to their ancestors, making offerings to Daoist gods and immortals at key festive days, and at the same time paying respects at the local Buddhist monastery.

The reason for this is that two of the three religions, Confucianism and Daoism, are both indigenous to China and so share a common "symbolic language" – to use Freedman's celebrated terminology – a language which is drawn from ancient Chinese culture, with its shamanic practices and correlative thinking.[2]

It often surprises people, for example, that Confucius refers more frequently to the Dao than either Lao Zi or Zhuang Zi do in their classics, and that one of the clearest early mentions of qi cultivation can actually be found in the work of another great Confucian philosopher, Mencius, earlier than such mentions occurred in many of the Daoist texts. Re-reading the classics of the Warring States period, it quickly becomes clear that Confucians believed in concepts such as the Dao and qi as much as the Daoists did, although they defined them in their own terms.

On the other hand, the earliest Daoist classics often mention Confucius and, although they are critical of Confucian positions, they still see value in them, and engage their rivals in a constructive debate. Zhuang Zi, for example, mentions Confucius more than he mentions Lao Zi and is always respectful in his criticisms of the older philosopher, at least in the Inner Chapters that are seen as having been written by Zhuang Zi himself.

It is later Han and post-Han Daoist literature, including later chapters added to the *Zhuang Zi* and later versions of the *Dao De Jing*, that see that early debate turn negative and ill tempered, reflecting the increased stakes as the two schools competed for political influence at the Imperial Court. It has been noted by scholars such as Kirkland, for example, that the earlier Guodian version of the *Dao De Jing* from circa 300 BC does not have any of the direct attacks on Confucians present in the later – and to us much more familiar – Mawangdui version from around 200 BC.[3]

The last of the three religions, Buddhism, is of course not indigenous to China, but one of its key branches, Chan Buddhism – or Zen, to use its more famous Japanese name – is, and it has absorbed within it much of the Chinese culture that the first Indian pilgrims would have encountered and had to accommodate.

As has already been mentioned, Chan Buddhism was influenced by the *Zhuang Zi* variant of Daoist thought, to such an extent that, to this day, the *Zhuang Zi* is seen as a core foundational text of their own tradition by many Chan masters. And of all types of Buddhism, it is Chan which has had the greatest influence on kung fu history, through the developments in the Shaolin Monastery.

Why is this link between the three religions important for the proper appreciation of kung fu philosophy? It is because there has never been a purely Buddhist or a purely Daoist style of kung fu. Some styles, for example Wudang or Shaolin, might associate more with one tradition or the other, but all styles share key concepts from across all three religions.

From Confucianism, all styles take the idea of filial piety that is so vital to the way kung fu is passed down from master to student. Buddhism has had a great influence on the ethics of martial arts, explaining when and how it is right to embrace violence.

Finally, Daoism, of all three, has had by far the greatest influence. It is from ancient Daoist practices that kung fu styles draw the ideas and techniques for qi cultivation.

These, as we have argued, separate kung fu from other styles of martial arts across the world and have also gone on to influence many other Asian martial arts, spreading in parallel to the spread of the three religions to Korea, Japan and Southeast Asia.

The Dao and the Pattern

The Dao is the single underlying principle in the Chinese world-view that is mentioned by all schools of philosophy, not just Daoists and Confucians, but also Yangists, Mohists, Legalists and others.

In the words of the *Dao De Jing*, "the Dao that can be spoken of, is not the Dao",[4] which of course presents a bit of a challenge to people like me who nonetheless want to speak of it.

The reason the Dao cannot be spoken of directly is because it can best be understood as the fundamental reality outside of human perception and subjectivity. As language itself is a subjective tool that we humans use to make sense of what we perceive, it would therefore be nonsensical to try to use language to describe what is outside language. In Ludwig Wittgenstein's words, "Whereof one cannot speak thereof one must be silent."[5]

Despite this, the greatest philosophers and poets, not only in China but across the world, have used the method of analogy, metaphor and poetic language to try to touch indirectly on what cannot directly be characterised. The objective is to bypass language and instead trigger a sensation or an image in the mind of the reader or listener, which gives them an idea of what the Dao might be, without trying to explain it literally.

The most common analogy for the Dao is that of a great river. The key thing this particular image tries to convey is that the Dao is not static, it changes and flows to its own unfathomable but entirely natural rhythms. The way to live your life, so this analogy goes on to imply, is to find these natural rhythms and go with them, as opposed to wasting energy swimming against the current. To all things in life, therefore, there is a natural position, to all problems a natural solution.

The Perfected Man (Shen Ren, literally "Spirit Man," as Zhuang Zi calls him) moves effortlessly and intuitively through the world, doing nothing specific but leaving nothing undone. This concept of action through inaction, or getting things done without trying to do anything, is a key concept of Daoism.

However, it is worth reading the *Dao De Jing* passage we quoted earlier in its entirety, to get the full sense of what is being conveyed here (too often people do not get beyond the first two lines in their quote and therefore miss a key understanding).

"The way that can be spoken of
Is not the constant way;
The name that can be named
Is not the constant name.
The nameless was the beginning of heaven and earth;
The named was the mother of the myriad creatures."[6]

The last line is no less important than the first, for it gives us a glimpse of how our world of perceptions arises from the immutable Dao: by the process of naming we build the reality around us. This is this and that is that and this is not that and that is connected to this. So, by the process of naming, we differentiate and build the correlative Pattern of the universe around us. After all, Wittgenstein also said, "The limits of my language mean the limits of my world."[7]

The Dao is still there behind the Pattern, and it has a rhythm to which the Pattern changes and moves and separates and then reconstitutes itself in a new configuration. We perceive the Pattern with our senses, but to be in tune with its changes, it is not the senses we have to use but our intuitive connection with the Dao.

The Pattern of the world around us is built up from the unity of the Dao via the interplay between the two primordial forces of Yin and Yang, which in turn support the trigram of Heaven, Earth and Man in between them and rotate through the cycle of the Five Elements of earth, wood, fire, water and metal, the eight trigrams and the sixty-four hexagrams. So, from one you get two, then three, then five, then eight, then sixty-four, then the ten thousand things, which, in Chinese meaning, signifies "everything".

Constructing the Pattern

Yin and Yang are the principles of duality that are necessary to differentiate one thing from another. Without a concept of duality, no Pattern can be built and so no reality can exist, or be perceived by us.

Yin is the dark side of the mountain, Earth (Di), coldness, water, the Moon, female, defence and retreat.

Yang is the light side of the mountain, Heaven (Tian), warmth, fire, the Sun, male, attack and advance.

Everything in the universe is said to consist of a particular blend of the two forces, and in traditional Chinese medicine, for example, illness is said to arise when a person's Yin and Yang are out of balance.

As the Pattern builds up in complexity, the next stage is the trigram of Heaven above, Earth below and Man in between connecting the two. This concept that a human being is able to act as a bridge between Heaven and Earth and channel the energy of both harks back to ancient shamanic ideas, where the shaman is able to rise up into the sky or descend into the depth of the Earth on his spirit journey, exploring places that are hidden from other men.

Beyond the cycle of the Yin and Yang, but connected to it, we have the cycle of the Five Elements. This is actually a much more recent principle than the dualistic Yin and Yang. According to textual evidence, the philosophy of the Five Elements was systematised by the Sage Zou Yan (Tsou Yen) around 350 BC from earlier traditions, but it was integrated into the canon during the Han Dynasty and has been a key part of the Chinese world-view ever since.

In the same way that everything in the world can be characterised by the balance of Yin and Yang within it, so everything can be defined in terms of the combination of the Five Elements:

- Earth is centre, late summer, sweet, yellow, stomach and spleen, ox, Saturn.
- Metal is west, autumn, acrid, white, lungs and large intestine, white tiger, Venus.

- Water is north, winter, salt, black, kidneys and bladder, black tortoise, Mercury.
- Wood is east, spring, sour, blue/green, dragon, liver and gall, Jupiter.
- Fire is south, summer, bitter, red, phoenix, heart and small intestine, Mars.[8]

One of the best as well as being one of the earliest expositions of the Five Elements, or the Five Phases as they are also called, can be found in the *Huai Nan Zi*, Chapter 4, "The Treatise on Topography:"

"Wood overcomes Earth, Earth overcomes Water, Water overcomes Fire, Fire overcomes Metal, Metal overcomes Wood...

When Wood is in its prime, Water is old, Fire is about to be born, Metal is paralyzed [imprisoned], and Earth is dead.

When Fire is in its prime, Wood is old, Earth is about to be born, Water is paralyzed, and Metal is dead.

When Earth is in its prime, Fire is old, Metal is about to be born, Wood is paralyzed, and Water is dead.

When Metal is in its prime, Earth is old, Water is is about to be born, Fire is paralyzed, and Wood is dead.

When Water is in its prime, Metal is old, Wood is about to be born, Earth is paralyzed, and Fire is dead.

In music there are five tones, of which the chief is gong.

There are five colours, of which the chief is yellow.

There are five flavours, of which the chief is sweet.

For positioning there are five materials (wucai), of which the chief is Earth.

This is why Earth when refined [subjected to change] produces Wood, Wood when refined produces Fire, Fire when refined produces clouds (of metallic qi), clouds when refined produce Water, and Water when refined reverts to Earth...

The five phases interact together, and so useful things are brought to completion."[9]

As we can see from this quotation, the Five Elements relate to each other in two ways: each one creates another and each one also destroys another.

Overlaid on top of the cycles of the Five Elements are the Ba Gua, the eight trigrams. These are based on ancient divination techniques using yarrow sticks, three in each trigram in a combination of straight and broken lines. These trigrams are then paired up to create sixty-four hexagrams used to foretell the future in the classic Chinese divination manual, the *Yi Jing*, or the *Book of Changes*, as has already been mentioned.

However, besides the direct use of the *Yi Jing* in foretelling the future, on a more esoteric level, it is used as a means of tracking the changes in the Pattern of the world caused by the flow and rhythm of the Dao. It is a road-map and a compass that a Sage can use to become a Perfected Man, in tune with the Dao

In this way the Yin and Yang, the Five Elements and the Ba Gua all serve the same purpose: in different ways and to different levels of detail, each describes the Pattern in an effort to understand it.

Applications in Kung Fu

This concept of the Pattern is of course fundamental to kung fu, for in kung fu, each taulu – each pattern – behaves as a microcosm of the greater Pattern of the world.

Reading this literally, each pattern is subject to the balance of hard and soft, the Yin and Yang, to the correct arrangement of the Five Elements which govern different types of movements, and to the sequence of the trigrams which are hidden in the posture of the body and the sequence of the steps, though how exactly these principles are applied is specific to the traditions of each style.

On a more symbolic level, the relationship between the Dao and the Pattern serves as a model for the relationship between two key principles in kung fu: control and spontaneity.

The Dao is formless and ever changing and cannot be pinned down. It is the essence of spontaneity, flexibility, effortlessness and naturalness. And yet from it comes the Pattern, the web of correlative interactions between all things. The Pattern is the essence of discipline, control; it is the principle behind taulu practice, where a set pattern of movements is passed down from generation to generation of martial artists.

The rules of filial piety, which we will explore in more detail later on, mean that it is possible for patterns to stay relatively unchanged over centuries, with modifications made by masters only rarely and with the utmost care, when a new discovery is made or a new insight is achieved. This is why the performance of a pattern is so important for martial arts practice. It is a ritual, an honouring of the ancestors of the style. From a person's pattern, a skilled martial artist can read their whole lineage and understand how that style being performed relates to their own style.

Yet the pattern cannot be rigid and lifeless. As my master often says, "you need to become your pattern and your pattern should become you." You internalise the principles of your style and from that point on, everything you do will always be your style. That is how it is possible to be spontaneous in movement and yet still be performing a recognisable style.

To master kung fu, you need both control and spontaneity, because they govern the balance of movement and stillness in patterns, the rhythms and timing in fighting, and the way set movements of taulu practice translate into sequences during fighting, enabling the kung fu practitioner to intuitively use the correct movements at the correct time. Spontaneously doing the right thing, spontaneously making the right choice, not being there when a blow lands.

This is what inexperienced practitioners so often get wrong. They see the fluid, relaxed, seemingly effortless movements of the master and try to copy them. But they do not understand that the fluidity is based upon years of disciplined practice of set patterns which have become internalised. The master no longer needs to think of what movement fits which situation, as the patterns he or she has practised will give them that without the need to apply thought. It is active thought that slows you down, makes you hesitate, makes your movements disjointed.

The student misses the point. It is not about fluidity and relaxation for their own sake; it is about doing the right thing at the right time. From the side, such rightness *looks* fluid and relaxed, but the latter is just a consequence of the former. Fluidity and relaxation without "rightness" are just so much pretty waving of arms and legs.

This intuitive translation of patterns into fighting is just the first step on the road. As we shall see in the next chapter, at the road's end, the fighter who is fully in tune with the Dao will not be there to fight at all.

Chapter 10

Man and Nature

This Chapter looks at different conceptions of the Perfected Man provided by the Daoist philosophers Lao Zi and Zhuang Zi, and considers to what extent being a Perfected Man is the objective of all internal cultivation, including the cultivation incorporated into kung fu.

All Chinese philosophic schools shared the view that man was intimately connected to nature, not just by virtue of being part of the natural world, sharing the land, sea and air with other living creatures, but on a more esoteric level by virtue of both man and everything else in existence being part of a single unified pattern, which was itself an expression of the indelible Dao.

Zhuang Zi

Among the philosophic schools, the Yangists and the Daoists gave particular emphasis to this understanding and its implications, and among the Daoists, Zhuang Zi stands head and shoulders above the rest in his eloquent, broad-ranging and profound explanation of this connection.

He was perhaps the greatest influence in establishing the symbolic tradition of the Daoist sage standing apart from the hustle and bustle of the human world and yet able to see straight into its heart, laying bare its inner workings. It is a symbolic tradition that forms an important and distinctive strand of Chinese philosophy, literature and art. That bittersweet, wistful, otherworldly, withdrawn but peaceful quality that permeates the poetry of Li Bai and Bai Ju Yi and the classical Chinese watercolours of mountain landscapes, not to mention later haiku and woodblock prints by Japanese masters, can be traced in no small way to the influence of Zhuang Zi.

Interestingly, if the tone, imagery and symbolism of Zhuang Zi have become all pervasive, the actual content of his teachings was largely misinterpreted by many later Daoist philosophers.

Zhuang Zi wrote of the importance of being in tune with nature, of not assigning undue importance to matters and concerns that were altogether artificial in his view. These included concerns such as wealth, political office, the whole range of social restrictions and expectations, the misunderstandings of language and miscommunication, and the fears and wants of our emotions, such as first and foremost our fear of death, which permeates everything else we do.

Zhuang Zi asked his readers to put such concerns in perspective when considering the great movements of the cosmos around us, and to treat with healthy scepticism anyone who tried to force us to act unnaturally based on overemphasising any particular ideology or artificial restriction. If we could summarise this approach to human life, it would be: Chill out, act by all means, if action is required, but keep things in perspective and never be out of step with the world.

Engagement with the World while Seeking Perfection

From what we know of Zhuang Zi from his own stories, he was never actually a recluse. He famously rejected the post of Prime Minister, valuing his privacy and his peace and quiet too much for such an office, but he seems to have lived in a normal community, a village or small town, had a wife he loved and had friends with whom he enjoyed debating and philosophising. The very act of him writing his book shows an engagement with human society, not a rejection of it.

This is one key area of misunderstanding of Zhuang Zi: too many later Daoists, while paying lip-service to him, turned to one excess or another: either living a life of strict asceticism and lonely seclusion, or creating cults with thousands of followers and seeking to meddle with the political organisation of the state. Zhuang Zi would have frowned upon either course of action.

Zhuang Zi extolled people to seek to become a Shen Ren, a phrase different scholars render variously as "Spirit Man", "Daemonic Man", or "Perfected Man". Although the first two renderings are closer to the literal sense, I think Zhuang Zi himself would have preferred the last one, "Perfected Man", as it best captures the sense that a Shen Ren is a man or woman who fully realises their human potential, which is given to all by nature but fully utilised only very rarely.

This Perfected Man is self-aware, connected to the rhythms of the universe, free of petty concerns that cloud the mind and dull the spirit, unafraid and unfettered by any conventions, and so free in the fullest sense of the word.

Zhuang Zi saw that self-perfection was possible through any human activity and certainly did not require one to be an ascetic dedicating your life to nothing but meditation on top of a mountain and far from other men.

He said of the Perfected Man:

"Such men as that had unremembering hearts, calm faces, clear brows. They were cool like autumn, warm like spring; they were pleased or angry evenly through the four seasons, did what fitted in with other things, and no one knew their high point."[1]

This means that the Perfected Man is such as and of himself and not through the trappings of being an ascetic, living apart from society. Because his state is internalised, he could do any job or activity that "fitted in with other things" without ever losing his perfected self.

Later on in the same chapter, Zhuang Zi is even more explicit:

"Someone in whom neither Heaven nor man is victor over the other, this is what is meant by the True Man."[2]

Zhuang Zi's view therefore can perhaps be understood as going further than saying that a Perfected Man *can* live fully engaged in society, but perhaps that he or she *should* do so, for it is part of human nature to be sociable and therefore if a Perfected Man stays true to his human nature, he will not fail to also be sociable.

Though of course *how* they choose to engage with society is not to be restricted just to roles and activities dictated by tradition, such as serving as ministers and generals. Zhuang Zi, for example, described Perfected Men who are able to set the kingdom to rights from afar, merely by the power of their spiritual essence. But the key thing is that they were still engaged and cared for the world they lived in and did not completely turn their backs on it.

Death, Immortality and Internal Cultivation

The other key area of misinterpretation is the relationship of the Perfected Man with death. Zhuang Zi saw death as a natural part of life, not something to be sought out before your time, but neither as something to be feared or avoided. He talked a lot about death, but only to affirm his childlike wonder at the awesome mysteries of life and the world around him, of which death was the greatest mystery of all:

"The True Men of old did not know how to be pleased that they were alive, did not know how to hate death, were neither glad to come forth nor reluctant to go in; they were content to leave as briskly as they came. They did not forget the source where they began, did not seek out the destination where they would end. They were pleased with the gift that they received, but forgot it as they gave it back."[3]

He would not have understood the obsessions with physical immortality that overwhelmed many later Daoist movements. He would have seen it as a futile attempt to fight against nature, against the Dao itself.

It is an open question whether Zhuang Zi would have objected to the alternative interpretation that immortality was to be sought in the freeing up and cultivation of the spirit rather than the physical preservation of the body. This spiritual rather than bodily immortality was the objective of many internal alchemists, or practitioners of nei dan, in Daoism, as we have seen in Parts 1 and 2 of this book.

Many later Daoists read evidence for such immortality of the spirit back into some passages of the *Zhuang Zi*, for example:

"The utmost man is daemonic... A man like that yokes the clouds to his chariot, rides the sun and moon and roams beyond the four seas; death and life alter nothing in himself, still less the principles of benefit and harm!"[4]

Though in reality, a passage such as this could just as easily mean that the Perfected Man is not altered by the *thought* of death, as much as that he is left somehow unchanged by the process of death itself.

Although either reading is possible in this and similar passages, I think Zhuang Zi's insight went further even than the idea of a spiritual rather than physical immortality.

For example, at one point, he criticises even Lie Zi (the putative author of the *Book of Lie Zi*) for hanging on to magic practices:

"...that Lieh-tzu now, he journeyed with the winds for his chariot, a fine sight it must have been, and did not come back for fifteen days. (Even so, there was something he failed to plant in his soil.)...even if he did save himself the trouble of going on foot, still depended on something to carry his weight. As for the man who rides a true course between heaven and earth, with the changes of the Six Energies for his chariot, to travel into the infinite, is there anything that he depends on?"[5]

For Zhuang Zi, even magic is something of the material world – depend on it too much and it becomes a barrier between the Perfected Man and the Dao, preventing the final unity with the Dao which should be the goal of every sage.

Puett interprets this, in my eyes correctly, as meaning that Zhuang Zi is warning against a complete abandonment of what it means to be human, in pursuit of special and magical powers:

"Gnosis is not a matter of transcending the human but of continuing and perfecting the Heaven within man... A spirit-man is not a man who becomes a spirit but a man who fully cultivates his spirit and thus wanders free from things while allowing things (including his own human form) to fulfil their natural endowment."[6]

So, the objective of the Perfected Man is not to achieve a magical or mystical power and through it perhaps immortality, becoming more like a spirit than a man, but rather to fully realise the human potential. If that leads to mystical powers, then fine, if it doesn't, then also fine. The mystical powers and immortality are not in themselves something to be sought because, as soon as they become that, then you cannot help but desire it and obsess over it, and so they will automatically become a fetter and a barrier, preventing you from becoming a fully Perfected Man.

This is an insight reminiscent of the Buddhist truth that to achieve Enlightenment, you have to let go of everything, even of Buddhism itself. Any kind of obsession is a fetter.

So, if any kind of immortality should be understood from the pages of the *Zhuang Zi*, it is not that death is physically or even magically avoided, but that death does not really exist in the way we perceive it. Nor, for that matter, does life.

That Zhuang Zi never states such things directly, but only hints at them through his use of metaphor, is due to the fact that he is sceptical about the disputations of other philosophers about the nature of reality, on the grounds that language confuses us when we try to use it to describe something that, by definition, lies outside of language and perception – the Dao.

For Zhuang Zi, "The Way comes about as we walk it,"[7] and a Perfected Man can achieve unity with it through his actions rather than being able to reason his way to an understanding of it.

This is Zhuang Zi's ultimate insight: there is only the Dao and its transformations, and it is only through actions that a man creates his own reality. Everything else may as well just be a dream:

> "Only at the ultimate awakening shall we know that this is the ultimate dream. Yet fools think they are awake, so confident that they know what they are, princes, herdsmen, incorrigible! You and Confucius are both dreams, and I who call you a dream am also a dream."[8]

The Dao De Jing

The other great Daoist classic, the *Dao De Jing*, is a hugely important and influential text, regardless of whether it was written by Lao Zi in the 6th century BC, which tradition would have us believe, or by some unnamed scholar in the 3rd century BC who tried to remain incognito and used the name of the mythical sage as his pen name – this is currently the most popular view of the academic community, as we discussed in Part 1.

Like the *Zhuang Zi*, the *Dao De Jing* also develops a theory of the

Perfected Man, though in this case, the focus is not on an individual's perfection for his or her own sake, but the ruler's perfection for the sake of the state and for the sake of his people.

Lao Zi's principal political teaching is that the Emperor or King should rule on the basis of De, which can be translated as "personal virtue and charismatic power". De measures the ability of the ruler to influence his subjects through his personal example.

However, the meaning of "De" goes deeper than just behaving in a way that inspires others to follow you. On a more transcendental level, the ruler needs to be in tune with the Dao, so all his actions and decisions are intuitively correct, and he exudes such a powerful sense of rightness and harmony that all people will work for the benefit of the state without having to be told or forced to do so:

"I take no action and the people are transformed of themselves;
I prefer stillness and the people are rectified of themselves;
I am not meddlesome and the people prosper of themselves;
I am free from desire and the people of themselves become simple like the uncarved block."[9]

Moreover, the De of the ruler will make even the forces of nature arrange themselves so as to benefit the state and the people:

"Should lords and princes be able to hold fast to it
The myriad creatures will submit of their own accord,
Heaven and earth will unite and sweet dew will fall,
And the people will be equitable, though no one so decrees."[10]

This understanding that a Perfected Man can use his virtue, De, to change the fate of the Empire and even affect the natural world is something that Lao Zi and Zhuang Zi share, only the latter refers to it as 'daemonic power', Shen, rather than De, but the effect is the same:

"In the mountains of far-off Ku-yi there lives a daemonic man, whose skin and flesh are like ice and snow... When the daemonic in him concentrates it keeps creatures free from plagues and makes the grain ripen every year."[11]

The difference between Lao Zi's use of De and Zhuang Zi's use of Shen is mainly the position of people who apply it, and more specifically whether or not they choose to live their lives in public.

Whereas you get the impression Zhuang Zi felt that the position of a leader, whether king, minister or general, would be counterproductive to the objective of becoming a Perfected Man, Lao Zi clearly saw things the other way around.

He taught that, as long as the ruler was able to keep himself free of details and small troubles of office, the action of ruling would not prevent him from practising self-cultivation. Quite the opposite; as long as the ruler stays in tune with the Dao, thereby increasing his personal virtue, his De, he will find his political dominion increase many fold:

"Lords and princes in virtue of the One become leaders in the empire."[12]

The disagreement between Zhuang Zi and Lao Zi, then, is about to what use you put your De, your charismatic and persuasive force: whether or not to deploy it in the political arena.

However, both are clear about where this power comes from: the unity of the man with the natural rhythms of the Dao.

Emptiness

The other key area Lao Zi discusses repeatedly in connection with ruling through De is the idea of emptiness. This seems to be a development of the instruction for the ruler to avoid meddling and unnecessary action, to the point that the ruler himself dissolves and becomes insubstantial:

"Thirty spokes
Share one hub.
Adapt the nothing therein to the purpose in hand, and you will
have the use of the cart. Knead clay in order to make a vessel.
Adapt the nothing therein to the purpose in hand, and you will
have the use of the vessel... Thus what we gain is Something,
yet it is by virtue of Nothing that this can be put to use."[13]

The emptiness of the hub makes the wheel a wheel and not the
spokes, which, without emptiness in the middle, will be just so many
planks of wood. The empty insides of a vessel make it what it is;
without it, the vessel will be just a lump of clay. These two metaphors would occur again and again in later Daoist thinking.

The rationale is that emptiness is the quality that is the closest to
the nature of the Way. So the practitioner needs to let go of his or her
fears, emotions, concerns and thoughts and empty their heart/mind
(xing). Only then would they achieve unity with the Way and with it
the state of Perfected Man.

Other famous metaphors in the *Dao De Jing* are the related imagery of water and femininity.

The female metaphor, whenever employed, is connected with
fruitfulness and nurturing – the "mother" archetype – but also with a
quiet inexhaustible strength, which is often read as an allusion to the
superior sexual stamina of the woman:

"The spirit of the valley never dies.
This is called the mysterious female.
The gateway of the mysterious female
Is called the root of heaven and earth.
Dimly visible, it seems as if it were there,
Yet use will never drain it."[14]

The water metaphor, like the female metaphor, is also used as an
example of nurturing:

"Highest good is like water. Because water excels in benefiting the myriad creatures without contending with them and settles where none would like to be, it comes close to the way."[15]

Both of these metaphors are used to advise the ruler to conquer through yielding, through softness and through emptiness, foregoing the harder and harsher masculine qualities of "action" and "aggression". And at times, the *Dao De Jing* is explicit on this matter, speaking plainly rather than through allusions:

"Turning back is how the way moves;
Weakness is the means the way employs.
The myriad creatures in the world are born from Something,
and Something from Nothing."[16]

Applications in Kung Fu

These ideas from the *Dao De Jing* and the *Zhuang Zi*, of emptiness, intuitive action, naturalness, calmness, femininity, the power of yielding, and influencing others by using persuasion and a charismatic power have all found application in kung fu.

These principles are particularly associated with internal styles such as Wudang Quan and Tai Ji Quan, but all kung fu styles, even those considered to be the most hard and external, for example southern Tiger styles, will have some measure of all these qualities.

Without some suppleness and softness inside, your body will be so rigid and slow as to be useless. Without some yielding in the course of a fight, you will be a one-dimensional fighter able only to attack and so easy to trick and lure into a trap. Without some quality of calmness, quietude and empty mind – the non attachment of wu wei – you will be so assailed by thoughts and emotions during a fight that you will be incapacitated. Without intuitiveness and naturalness in movement, you will be too slow to react to the changing rhythm of your opponent.

Although these ideas may be derived from two Daoist classics, they apply equally to all styles of kung fu, including the ones with Buddhist heritage, as we have seen.

However, just as with the Yin and Yang, Five Elements and Eight Trigrams we discussed in the previous chapter, the more important influence the *Zhuang Zi* and the *Dao De Jing* classics have on kung fu philosophy is not the literal influence on the way you fight. Rather it is on the way you, as a martial artist and practitioner of kung fu, should live.

In Part 1, we examined how the internal cultivation practices taught in the *Neiye*, a classic written at more or less the same time as the *Zhuang Zi*, have become an inseparable part of kung fu.

When we look at the teachings of Zhuang Zi and Lao Zi, we begin to see why these cultivation practices are important for a kung fu practitioner and what their ultimate purpose is. It is to make the absolute most we can of our human abilities, honing our mind, body and spirit to the maximum level nature granted us, because the Perfected Man is not a spirit or a magician, but is a human being who has fully realised his natural powers.

According to both Zhuang Zi and Lao Zi, these powers are considerable indeed, allowing the Perfected Man to influence people and events effortlessly; to be so in tune with the cosmos that it would seem to an onlooker that even the forces of nature themselves bend to his will. Of course, in reality, the Perfected Man simply knows and uses their natural rhythms.

It is through such intuitive knowledge that a Perfected Man ensures that they are not there to fight at all, if they do not choose to do so – which is the absolute goal of self-defence, as we have mentioned in the last chapter – for they are the master of every situation, surprised by nothing, never flustered, never on the back foot, always intuitively making the right choice.

To lead the kind of life Zhuang Zi describes is to understand what it means to be fully human. It is at the same time the greatest challenge and the most natural thing in the world.

As we shall see in Chapter 13, the model of the Perfected Man shows us how kung fu can and should be applied to our life as a whole rather than to the hours we spend honing our martial skills. Kung fu at its root is more than the art of fighting. It is the art of living.

Chapter 11

Man and Society

This Chapter considers two of the most important principles of the martial arts: filial piety and brotherhood, both of which are derived from Confucian philosophy rather than from Daoism, but as the chapter concludes by saying, there are no contradictions between the two sets of ideas.

If Daoism bequeathed to kung fu the principle of intuitiveness and oneness with the world and the nei gong exercises that underpin our internal strength training, then Confucianism gave kung fu a no less important and far-reaching principle: filial piety, the relationship between a master and a student, the inheritance of a style from your ancestors, the ethics and discipline of practice and the ideas of brotherhood and camaraderie. Without all of these principles, kung fu practice would be too dangerous a power for an individual to wield.

Filial Piety and the Difference between China and the West

The relationship of filial piety is fundamentally patterned on the relationship between father and son, which Confucius saw as the way all relationships should be conducted, including that between a ruler and his subjects and a teacher and his students.

In Confucius' own words, from the opening page of *The Analects*:

"...Those who in private life behave well towards their parents and elder brothers, in public life seldom show a disposition to resist the authority of their superiors. And as for such men starting a revolution, no instance of it has ever occurred. It is upon the trunk that a gentleman works. When that is firmly set up, the Way grows. And surely proper behaviour towards parents and elder brothers is the trunk of Goodness?"[1]

This passage might sound oddly conformist to a modern Western reader. That is because the Chinese understanding of an individual's place in society is fundamentally different to that of the West.

In the West, at least since the Age of Enlightenment, individualism and the rights pertaining to an individual are seen as paramount. In fact, these rights are described as "universal" human rights. Democracy as a system of government is designed to ensure such rights, giving each citizen an equal say in what happens, regardless of their wealth, status or merit.

Obviously this is an oversimplification. Wealth, status and merit no doubt all give different weight to the influence of different individuals in the course of everyday life outside the special and very limited circumstances of general elections or referenda. Nonetheless, at least the intention of equality between citizens is there, woven into the fabric of Western societies.

A Confucian would make a very simple but nonetheless very powerful critique of this approach: in counting the views of current generations, how do we make sure we do not ignore the views of the generations that preceded us and of generations that will follow?

If the generations who are now dead and so cannot vote made sacrifices to build something, what right do we now have to tear it down, even if we vote for that action in the majority? Furthermore, how do we avoid prioritising our short-term interest over longer term goals? So, if an action might lead to a good outcome in two hundred years' time, would it ever have a chance of being voted through now, if it comes with short-term pain for the duration of the voters' lives? A valid question indeed at the time of the current Climate Change debate.

Without considering this interesting point much further in this book, I would argue that this alternative view of human society, as continuous through generation after generation, with the interests of all generations having to be included in a decision, should at least make us in the West challenge our own assumptions.

Filial Piety in Kung Fu

Where this has influence on the practice of kung fu is the importance attached to the transmission of knowledge from master to student through generations, and the implications this transmission has for the behaviour of both master and student.

The key insight is that all of us, in addition to being individuals with our own wants and needs, strengths and weaknesses, prejudices and beliefs, are simultaneously links in a chain of transmission, both of our genes from our parents, and of knowledge and skills from our teachers.

If we should decide not to procreate or do not take our responsibility as parents seriously, letting our children perish, then our genetic line will die out and all the trials and tribulations of previous generations of our ancestors would come to nought. Likewise, if we do not learn diligently and then teach responsibly, our style will not survive. Once the knowledge is extinguished, it can never be fully recreated and, at that point, all the sacrifices of generations of practitioners before us would become meaningless.

If you stop for a moment and think about it, you realise what a tremendous burden of expectations and responsibilities we all carry. That is why Confucius placed so much importance in his teachings on the relationship between father and son and teacher and student.

Each of these relationships represents a link in the chain of transmission and a hope of survival in the future.

Students in the modern day (in the West, but also increasingly in China itself) often question the perceived inequality of the relationship between master and student and fight against it.

This is understandable, and I doubt the situation was much different one or two thousand years ago. It is a natural by-product of the tension between our two roles: of an individual in our own right, an independent agent, and as a link in a chain between past and future generations. It is felt more acutely today for the simple reason that, in our more comfortable lives, we are simply too unused to discipline and sacrifice.

And, on the surface, the relationship between master and student in kung fu does seem unequal. What the master says, the student is expected to do without question, whether they agree with it or not. The student is expected to sacrifice their rights and freedoms willingly and rearrange their whole life in pursuit of excellence. For all of us born in the modern world, particularly in the West, accepting this is a challenge.

However, looking more deeply, this Confucian model does have an internal balance of its own, for, just as the burden of discipline is on the student, the burden of responsibility is on the master. This is the responsibility to teach well, to transmit the style and care for your students. In the Confucian world-view, each failure of each student rests heaviest on the teacher, for it means that they have not taught their student correctly, just as the failure of the son would bring dishonour to the father, and the failure of the state would lose the Emperor his mandate to rule, given by Heaven.

The discipline required of the student and the responsibility required of the master are both key to enabling the transmission of knowledge and skill to take place. Kung fu, after all, is an art that gives its practitioner great power over others, those who do not practise. Discipline from the student is required to make sure they do not misuse their abilities. And the weight of responsibility needs to be on the teacher to make sure they take due care in who they choose to teach: once they become your student, there is no washing your hands of them. Even if a student leaves the teacher, the latter is still responsible for the former's conduct.

Finally, it is important to remember that the teaching of kung fu can never be forced on an individual. Filial piety does not require that free will is suspended. Quite the opposite. It is an important part of its power that both actors freely choose to accept their particular burden: the teacher his responsibility and the student his discipline. This is something that modern generations often find difficult to understand: rights actually limit you as a human being with free will, because they are given and enforced by a third party such as the State or the Court, not won for oneself. On the other hand, duties and responsibilities make you grow as a human being because you have to freely choose to take them on. In this way, they are empowering.

By this understanding, the relationship between master and student is one of different positions in the pattern, but of equal power. The master may be the one issuing instructions, but at the core of it the student chooses freely to submit and, by doing so, is himself empowered. When the pattern changes, it is the student's turn to accept responsibility for taking on students and teaching them well.

The actions of both master and student in applying the rules of filial piety and managing the transmission of the style is underpinned by the imperative of the style to survive and be passed on to the next generation at least as strong as it was passed to them.

However, this imperative needs to be counterbalanced by the idea of benevolence. Students cannot do wrong and excuse themselves by saying that their master told them to do so; and the master cannot do wrong and excuse himself by saying that his responsibility to the style forced him to do so.

Explanation of Benevolence

The idea of benevolence goes right back to the Confucian view that all filial piety based relationships, as the name implies, are patterned on the primal relationship between a parent and a child, and that relationship is by nature founded on love and benevolence.

Sarah Allan, for example, explains that:

"Human society, in Confucius' view, was based on the instinctive love between children and their parents. Filial piety thus became... the offering of love and respect to one's parents, and by extension to all elders and superiors. Conversely, parents also love and nurture their children and this relationship was the model for good government."[2]

To work, therefore, the filial relationship must be based on mutual love and hence mutual benevolence, the intention to do good by each other.

With the correct application of responsibility and discipline and with benevolence guiding the actions of both the master and the student, the application of filial piety is able to work as intended, allowing the transmission of the style and so its survival into the future. However, with any of these elements missing, the correct relationship will break down and then the rules of filial piety can be opened to abuse.

This can best be understood using an archetypal example of filial piety in Chinese history: the story of Marshal Yue Fei that we considered in Chapter 7.

Yue Fei can be said to have fulfilled the requirements of filial piety to the utmost by obeying the imperial edict to pull his forces back on the eve of a possible victory over the Jin.

As such, he acted as the perfect subject to his Emperor, in the Confucian view. The Emperor, however, failed to show benevolence by not preventing Yue Fei's death. Through that failure, the Emperor undermined his own mandate to rule and was only able to survive the retribution of his people by repenting publicly and sacrificing the people who advised him to execute Marshal Yue Fei: the prime minister and his luckless wife.

The passions still stirred by the curse of the prime minister have at their root a failure of benevolence to balance out the strictures of filial piety.

The Ideal of Brotherhood

Beyond the teacher/student relationship and the responsibility and discipline that comes with it, another key relationship is between students to each other. That is based on a separate Confucian relationship of older brother to younger brother.

Students who train together go through shared pain and hardship. This bonds them together and creates a sense of camaraderie, of brotherhood based on a principle that the Chinese call "Yi", which can be translated variously as "appropriateness", "responsibility", "duty", "self-sacrifice" or "honour". It also forms part of the phrase "jieyi", literally "binding honour," which is the phrase used to describe the taking of an oath of brotherhood.[3]

Yi is a core Confucian principle that guides the behaviour of a man to make sure it is always appropriate and honourable. In a way, Yi is the Confucian version of that quality that, for Daoists, makes one a Perfected Man: it is the intuitive unity between a man and the Dao. It is just that, for Confucians, this unity was enacted in ritual behaviour and a strict adherence to the examples of behaviour set by the ancestors. By contrast, Daoists, at least in early classics such as the *Zhuang Zi* and the *Dao De Jing*, de-emphasised ritual.

This bond of brotherhood based on Yi is most famously embodied in the relationship of the heroes of *the Romance of the Three Kingdoms*: Liu Bei, Zhang Fei and Guan Yu, the Brothers of the Peach Orchard.

They swore themselves –"jieyi"– to each other in a peach orchard when all three were young men, and what united them was a fervent wish to help protect and restore the Han Empire which, at the time, was under attack from rebels and suffering from corruption at court.

This act carried them through years of wars fought side-by-side and numerous victories and defeats. In the end, they failed to unify the Empire, but managed to restore the Han Dynasty embodied by Liu Bei himself in one corner of the Empire, in the kingdom of Shu Han.

At this point of great success, the throne occupied by one of the brothers and at least the opportunity to win back the rest of the Empire still open to them, one of the brothers, Guan Yu, was captured and executed.

Here, an interesting development occurred which shows the possible friction between filial piety and the principle of Yi: filial piety would have said that Liu Bei's greater responsibility was to continue to restore the Empire from his base in Shu Han. However, he disregarded the advice of his strategist Zhuge Liang and chose instead to take revenge for his brother's death, by attacking the kingdom of his brother's executioner, Sun Quan.

For Liu Bei, then, Yi was in the final calculation even more important than filial piety and he knowingly sacrificed the Empire for his brother's memory. Doing so caused the eventual defeat of Shu Han and the death of all three brothers, but it also won them an immortality arguably far greater than if they had succeeded in unifying the Empire under their rule. Instead of holding the Throne of Heaven, they ascended to Heaven themselves, all three being deified by later generations as gods, Lord Guan most famously becoming the God of War.[4]

We might ask how Yi, a more junior relationship in the Confucian sense, can triumph over filial piety in this way?

The answer is that filial piety is itself junior in the Chinese worldview to the changes dictated by the Dao, and when the time comes for the dynasty to fall, having lost the Mandate of Heaven, then it will fall. In such times, the filial piety obligations to restore it would be naturally weakened. The obligations of the brothers to each other, however, were independent of the state of the Empire, resting on their loyalty and honour. Therefore, Liu Bei acted intuitively and in tune with the Way by prioritising Yi over a weakened obligation, through filial piety, to restore a dynasty whose time had come and whose mandate had passed. In the Daoist sense, he acted as a Perfected Man, whose decisions are always right, coming as they do intuitively from the heart.

The importance of brotherhood in kung fu philosophy is that it is seen as the glue that binds martial artists together through the hardships of their training and the dangers of warfare.

Without brotherhood, soldiers would find it impossible to face the horrors of war, as it is for their friends and for their brothers in arms that they are willing to put themselves in danger, thus overriding the otherwise overpowering human instinct of self-preservation.

During the Qing Dynasty, it was the sense of brotherhood, heightened by the racist policies of the Manchu government towards the Han Chinese, that fuelled the flowering of martial arts and the creation of numerous secret societies. The fist-in-hand salute, that has now been adopted almost universally by martial artists across Asia, has the double meaning of "brothers united" (the fist representing the five brother monks who escaped the burning of the Shaolin Monastery, the hand on top uniting them) and "Overthrow the Qing, support the Ming" (the fist and open hand together representing the character for "Ming" as the name of the last indigenous Chinese dynasty).

In this way, every time a martial arts practitioner performs that salute today, they reaffirm the principle of kung fu brotherhood, often without realising it.

Confucian versus Daoist Ideas

One might ask how these Confucian ideas of filial piety and benevolence relate to the Daoist ideas discussed earlier. How can the philosophy of kung fu accommodate both?

The answer is that there is no inherent contradiction between them. Let's take the example of the practice of internal cultivation of the *Neiye*, which we have argued is crucial to kung fu. A quick look at the Confucian classics shows that Confucian ideas sit quite happily alongside such practices.

As we have already mentioned briefly, the great Confucian philosopher Mencius talked about developing "flood-like qi" in his classic the *Meng Zi*, notwithstanding that later Confucian scholars tried to make him out as a great opponent of heterodox traditions such as Daoism.

Russell Kirkland points out that there are actually a number of parallels between the *Meng Zi* and the *Neiye*, as both agree on three key points:

> "1. One is born with a heart/mind that is inherently as it should be;
> 2. Our heart/mind became confused as our thoughts and passions intensified; and
> 3. by returning our heart/mind to its original qualities, we allow a natural harmony to take the place of unnatural confusion."[5]

Kirkland thus makes a point that there may be a deeper affinity between the Confucian position of someone like Mencius and the early practitioners of internal cultivation than just a single mention of qi. Rather they had a shared view of the development and nature of man.

This same view is also taken by Roth, who mentions Mencius and his connection with the *Neiye*, but also mentions that the other great Warring States Confucian, Xun Zi, was also "aware of these inner cultivation methods and even advocated them."[6]

To support his statement, Roth quotes the following line in the *Xun Zi*:

> "...of all the methods of regulating the vital breath and nourishing the mind, none is more direct than proceeding

according to ritual principles, none more essential than obtaining a good teacher, and none more intelligent than unifying one's likes."[7]

From the tone and manner in which Xun Zi discusses cultivation techniques, it is quite clear that he saw them as widespread and not in need of special introduction. In fact, his emphasis is on how best to apply them and use them, rather than on whether they are useful as a practice at all – the latter is treated as a given.

Roth also points out that there is a whole page in the *Neiye* itself which shows clear Confucian influence:

"As for the vitality of all human beings:
It inevitably occurs because of balanced and aligned [breathing].
The reason for its loss
Is inevitably pleasure and anger, worry and anxiety.
Therefore, to bring your anger to a halt, there is nothing better than poetry;
To cast off worry there is nothing better than music;
To limit music there is nothing better than the rites;
To hold onto the rites there is nothing better than reverence;
To hold onto reverence there is nothing better than tranquillity.
When you are inwardly tranquil and outwardly reverent
You are able to return to your innate nature
And this nature will become greatly stable."[8]

As this is the only passage, as Roth mentions, which has such overtly Confucian ideas as rites and music, it may well be a later addition to the *Neiye* text, but that does not invalidate the point. Its inclusion in the classic shows that either the early Daoists engaged with Confucian ideas, or that the later Confucians added this passage into a Daoist text, thus engaging with Daoist ideas. Either way, there is no inherent contradiction between Confucianism and internal cultivation.

Much the same can be said about the second key Daoist concept that forms part of kung fu philosophy: that of becoming a Perfected Man.

The Lao Zi version of what it means to be a Perfected Man was accepted by Confucian scholars early on, with the political ideas of the *Dao De Jing* being quoted by Xun Zi and many other later Confucian scholars.

One might think that Zhuang Zi's apolitical definitions of Shen Ren would be less easy to reconcile with Confucianism and ideas of filial piety and benevolence, but here we can use the *Zhuang Zi* classic itself as evidence. In one of the inner chapters that academics ascribe to Zhuang Zi himself, he relates with apparent approval the following teaching of Confucius:

> "'In the world there are two supreme commandments,' said Confucius. 'One of them is destiny, the other duty. A child's love of his parents is destined: it cannot be dispelled from the heart. A minister's service to his lord is duty; wherever he may go his lord is his lord. The commandments from which there is no escape between heaven and earth, these are what I call the supreme ones. This is why in the service of parents there is no higher degree of filial conduct than to live contentedly wherever they may dwell, in the service of a lord no fuller measure of loyalty than to perform his tasks contentedly whatever they may be, and in the service of one's own heart no higher degree of Power than, without joy and sorrow ever alternating before it, to know that these things could not be otherwise, and be content with them as our destiny.'"[9]

This statement – at first glance very un-Daoist – which for that reason is rarely quoted by partisan scholars of either the Daoist or Confucian camps who try too hard to avoid any statements that might contradict their views – is nonetheless in perfect accord with Zhuang Zi's other beliefs in acting naturally and not being fettered.

What Zhuang Zi is saying, using Confucius as his mouthpiece, is that a Perfected Man can be free even when he is outwardly constrained by conventions. Some things are just meant to be, and there is no point fighting them, any more than there is a point in fighting natural forces of wind or fire. In these circumstances, it is entirely natural to go with convention, but a Perfected Man does so without feeling forced or fettered: it is just the natural thing to do.

Angus Graham notes in his analysis of this chapter that:

"Chuang-tzu does not question the institutions of family and state, although he does not talk about them much. You do in the last resort acknowledge a duty to the state in which you live, and if by choice or necessity you come to be in office you accept its rules as belonging to the 'inevitable'. However narrow the limits, as long as you preserve the responsiveness of your energies you can still... 'roam free inside the cage'."[10]

This analysis shows that even Zhuang Zi's apolitical definition of the Perfected Man is not necessarily inconsistent with Confucian ideas of filial piety and benevolence, allowing both to be blended into the philosophy of kung fu.

Chapter 12

Violence, Warfare and Kung Fu

This chapter starts off by examining some of the key texts of the military strategists and then considers how the ethical dimension of the martial arts can be reconciled with their core objective of committing violence against another being.

Considerations of the philosophy and cultural heritage that underpin kung fu should not confuse us as to its fundamental nature. It is a *martial* art, and as such it is about war, violence and aggression and our ability as individuals to control and channel those destructive forces that are an inevitable part of human nature.

The *Art of War* tradition

Since warfare is so integral to the human experience, Chinese theorists have unsurprisingly excelled in the theory of warfare itself. Numerous classic texts have been produced over three millennia of Chinese history, which dealt with how war should be waged to gain victory.

The oldest such text is Jiang Ziya's *Six Secret Teachings* from the beginning of the Zhou Dynasty (though the text itself was likely written during the Warring States period, taken from earlier Zhou sources). However, the most famous are undoubtedly the two separate texts called *The Art of War*, by Sun Wu (more often referred to as Sun Zi, literally Master Sun) and his descendant Sun Bin, and the many related works written as commentaries or elaborations of these classics by later historical luminaries such as the Three Kingdoms warlord Cao Cao and his rival strategist Zhuge Liang.

At first glance, these texts deal with warfare on the scale of armies moving and facing off in the field, and states preparing themselves for war, rather than on the smaller scale of the individual fighter and his training, preparation and fighting strategies.

However, there is no shortage of modern and ancient texts that seek to apply the principles to different areas of human activity, from commerce to politics.

It is also common for writers about particular styles of kung fu to extrapolate the principles of Sun Zi or Sun Bin, and apply them to the fighting strategies of an individual fighter. It is not difficult to see how, say, Sun Zi's stratagems can be used to teach a fighter the key lessons of correct timing of attack and defence, dominating and making the best use of the space in the ring, the psychological impact of fear or surprise, or the usefulness of pretence and subterfuge to manipulate your opponent's responses.

However, there is one aspect of the strategy classics that has been missed by many commentators, and that is considering to what extent military strategy itself is a kind of kung fu.

Military Strategy as Kung Fu

As mentioned in Chapter 2, whereas the individual fighter uses his hands and feet and then learns to use weapons such as spear and sword as an extension of his body and hands, so a strategy master goes a step further and uses as his weapons other men's bodies and minds in the order of thousands upon thousands. If you see the classics in this light, you can begin to appreciate that the great military strategists were in fact practising their own very particular kung fu.

Secondly, practised at the highest level, the arts of military strategy incorporate many of the Daoist ideas we have discussed in previous chapters as being an integral part of kung fu. This includes mention of concepts such as qi, the Dao, Yin and Yang, the Five Elements and, most particularly, the trigrams of the *Yi Jing* throughout the classics.

However, this might just point to a common symbolic language gradually shared by all Chinese philosophies. A more important area of overlap with Daoist self-cultivation ideas is that the strategy classics themselves teach that the highest-level strategists achieve a state similar to that of Zhuang Zi's Perfected Man.

They are able to internalise the working of the Cosmos and the Dao, to arrive at intuitively correct decisions on the battlefield as things change and develop around them. Zhuge Liang in his own military classic describes this state as "harmonising with changes":

"The art of certain victory, the mode of harmonizing with changes, is a matter of opportunity. Who but the perspicacious can deal with it? And of all avenues of seeing opportunity, none is greater than the unexpected."[1]

Zhuge Liang's "perspicacious" generals seem to be those who are the most attuned with the Pattern and the changes of the Dao.

Sun Zi describes a similar state achieved by the greatest strategists in order to deal with the chaos of battle:

"To face confusion with composure and face clamour with calm is mastery of heart."[2]

It is this calm mastery of changing events that most readily recalls the abilities of a Perfected Man, achieved through self-cultivation.

Sun Bin, in his *Art of War*, perhaps gives the most defining description of this state, using the word "sages" to describe those strategists who are able to achieve it:

"...the sages know how to use the characteristics of things to overpower them, and there are inexhaustible ways of overpowering things and controlling situations. War is a contest between dispositions seeking to prevail over one another... The question is whether you always know the right method to use to overpower a particular disposition. The changes in the mutual checks among things in the world are as everlasting as heaven and earth and truly inexhaustible."[3]

To my mind, there are clear affinities between these ideas in strategy classics and the Daoist ideas discussed earlier.

As a final piece of evidence to support this theory, it is worth remembering that there were Daoist versions of military classics being produced, that blended the ideas of nei gong with those of such teachers as Sun Wu and Sun Bin. In Chapter 4, we quoted from one such classic, the military strategy chapter of the *Huai Nan Zi*, and demonstrated the integral place of that work in the history of the development of kung fu.

For all these reasons, I would argue that strategy in the Warring States and other periods when it was at its height *was* a kind of kung fu in its own right. A kung fu of a type that used armies as its weapons, and that valued the abilities of its masters to achieve the kind of state of mind, calm and still, that is valued in other Daoist practices that we have considered elsewhere. The strategy classics did not advise on how such a state of mind could be achieved, but the popularity of nei gong and related "hygiene" practices of Peng Zu at the time classics like Sun Bin's *Art of War* were being written, as we saw in Chapter 3, would at least make it possible that this was done via similar methods of self-cultivation.

The Morality of Martial Arts

As we have seen, a lot of kung fu culture is closely connected to religious practice, both Daoism and Buddhism. This raises a key question about how to reconcile the violence and aggression inherent in martial practice with the morality required by religion.

First of all, we need to understand that Buddhism and Daoism each bring a different kind of morality to kung fu. In Daoism, violence is a natural part of experiencing the world, both natural and supernatural. One of the symbols of Daoist priests is the straight sword. This is because an important role of the priests was to fight and vanquish evil spirits to protect their community. Magic weapons and amulets are part of the arsenal for the Daoist priest.

Furthermore, because so many things, both good and bad, happen naturally in the world, including injury, illness, poverty and death, Daoists have little in the way of prescriptive or normative morality. "Thou shalt" and "thou shalt not" are not part of the Daoist lexicon. For this reason, many rival philosophers, including the Confucians in China and humanist and Christian thinkers in the West, have often characterised Daoism as immoral or at best amoral.

I do not believe that this is a very accurate representation. Reading Lao Zi's *Dao De Jing*, you are struck first with a deep-seated concern for the well being of the citizens of the state. Lao Zi repeatedly exhorts the Emperor to be a good ruler. He does not do so by means of rituals and regulations like the Confucians, nor by means of discipline and punishments like the Legalists, but rather by nurturing the Emperor's personal charismatic force, the De. However, a key part of that De is benevolence and compassion:

"I have three treasures
Which I hold and cherish.
The first is known as compassion,
The second is known as frugality,
The third is known as not daring to take the lead in the empire;
Being compassionate one could afford to be courageous,
Being frugal one could afford to extend one's territory,

Not daring to take the lead in the empire one could afford to be lord over the vessels."[4]

With regards to warfare, Lao Zi clearly believed that it was a failure of De on the part of the ruler to get themselves involved in war. However, he accepted that it was sometimes unavoidable:

"Arms are instruments of ill omen, not the instruments of the gentleman. When one is compelled to use them, it is best to do so without relish. There is no glory in victory, and to glorify it despite this is to exult in the killing of men. One who exults in the killing of men will never have his way in the empire."[5]

Lao Zi makes it clear how a Perfected Man should behave in war:

"One who is good [at the art of war] aims only at bringing his campaign to a conclusion and dare not thereby to intimidate... Bring it to a conclusion but do not be arrogant; bring it to a conclusion but only when there is no choice..."[6]

This teaching can apply just as surely to the behaviour of a martial artist: if you can, avoid the fight; if you cannot avoid it, then do the minimum required to win, without relishing the aggression the fight brings up.

Zhuang Zi, on the other hand, does not concern himself with matters of state, but his writing too is suffused with a profound sympathy for the plight of the common man, advising him to be a "useless tree" from which no wood can be made, meaning to keep himself away from the troubled times and the ever-hungry need of the state to make use of its citizens, whether conscripting them into armies or taxing them to within an inch of their lives. We need to remember how violent the times were during the Warring States period when Zhuang Zi was alive to fully appreciate this sentiment.

So, both Lao Zi and Zhuang Zi, the greatest Daoist masters, show sympathy and concern for their fellow citizens. In other words, they show compassion, which is after all at the root of any moral system. It is just that they refuse to take the next step and, in the name of compassion, try to regulate the lives of those same citizens – in the Daoist view, this meddling is unnatural.

After Lao Zi and Zhuang Zi, some Daoists did try to engage with ethics and morality, for example the sect of Zhang Dao Ling, who created a state within a state in China, with its own rules, among which incidentally was one of the earliest attempts at true equality between men and women, and between rich and poor. Other Daoists continued to follow Lao Zi and Zhuang Zi and concern themselves with cultivating the individual rather than producing moral rules. However, compassion was always part of the Daoist idea of the Perfected Man.

In the eyes of Daoist martial artists, I would argue therefore there was no contradiction between feeling compassion for fellow men and understanding and accepting the naturalness of the violent impulses that sometimes drive us.

Buddhist Compassion and Non-violence

For Buddhists, the seeming tension between the violence that is inherent to martial arts and their religious doctrine is much more acute. Buddhism, after all, originally came out of Indian culture, and from these roots, it inherited the principle of non-violence or Ahimsa. This means that a devout Buddhist will avoid taking another life for fear of incurring bad karma.

The principle of compassion in Buddhism is also much stricter than the Daoist interpretation, as it is not leavened by the insight that certain types of violence, aggression, competition and the like are natural to the world and so cannot be artificially managed away.

Buddhists believe rather that human life is at its core a life of suffering. Moreover, it is unnecessary suffering, for it only arises because human beings are under the illusion that their life and the world around them are real and therefore that the suffering is real, whereas in fact it is not. It is the goal of every Buddhist to perceive this truth, thus reaching Enlightenment, and in the process of attempting this, they must not add to the illusion of suffering that already exists through any acts such as violence or warfare. The question then arises of how it is even possible to have a Buddhist martial art?

The answer that Buddhists come up with is both pragmatic and profound: you can only raise arms in defence of others, particularly those who are weaker than you, and cannot defend themselves. In doing so, you still tie yourself more deeply into the illusion of Samsara (the percieved world of suffering), but you do so willingly for the good of others. In fact, this is where the idea of a Bodhisattva comes from; a saintly being who knowingly forsakes their final release from Samsara out of compassion for others, so that they might help them.

This restriction on the use of violence for self-defence only has since become integral to all martial arts ethics. In practice, of course, what constitutes self-defence and what is pure aggression is a difficult judgement. For Buddhists, it is a judgement ultimately made through the mechanism of karma, which no individual can deceive as to their most private motivation in committing an act of violence. To avoid accidentally going further than intended and thereby incurring bad karma, Buddhist martial artists have consciously sought to minimise the damage they can do, for example, by adapting non-lethal weapons such as a staff, instead of sharp steel.

Channelling Latent Violence to Positive Effect

Since most if not all styles of kung fu practised today have been influenced by all three of the great religions of China as part of the general inheritance of Chinese culture, they tend to subscribe to a mixture of both ideas at the same time: the Daoist one that violence is natural but must be balanced by compassion and benevolence, and the Buddhist one that martial arts can only be used in self-defence. And, as we have already seen, to these two ideas is added the third, Confucian one: that of the need for filial piety as a way to make sure that students are taught correctly of their responsibilities, before releasing to them any skill that they might misuse to harm others.

This three-part approach to kung fu ethics allows us to reconcile ourselves with the negative and destructive aspects of kung fu's latent violence. It is sufficient at a time of war, when kung fu's obvious benefits in arming yourself against the violence of others and so protecting yourself, your loved ones and your property, are clear. But what about a time of peace, as many of us are fortunate enough to enjoy in the West today, at the start of the 21st century? What reason do we have to study kung fu as a martial art and take on the burden of responsibility it entails during a time of peace?

This brings us back to Daoism and its teaching of the need to act naturally and let the Dao move as it will.

This was never intended to be an example of some sort of absolute relativism, where all outcomes are natural and therefore equally good. As we have seen, although violence is part of nature in the way, for example, animals have to kill other animals for food, Daoist masters nonetheless argued for compassion. So they expressly did not believe that a person picking up an axe and killing his neighbour with no provocation was a neutral outcome compared to them, say, helping their neighbour in need. For Daoists, the latter behaviour is better than the former, so although the instinct to violence might be natural, the act of violence is not to be desired unless there is a good reason for it.

This interpretation of Daoism is evident in the debate between Robert Eno and Michael Puett. Eno, in his essay *Cook Ding's Dao and the Limits of Philosophy*, states that "Dao-practices can be adapted to any end: the Dao of butchering people might provide much the same spiritual spontaneity as the Dao of butchering oxen – as many a samurai might testify." This is an extreme consequence of the thought that it is the process of gaining and exercising supreme skill that is important for Daoists, not any ethical consequence of it.

Puett, however, says that though a philosopher like Zhuang Zi might not assign importance to ethics, nonetheless he would not think that "butchering" people was equally acceptable to other actions. According to Puett, "Zhuangzi is asserting that the cultivated human spirit acts in certain ways rather than others. He does so not by asserting that particular activities are ethically better than others but by making a cosmological claim: the truly human person will inherently behave in certain ways rather than in other ways."[7]

A Perfected Man would be able to avoid having to commit violence, by controlling his instinct for aggression and channelling it into something more constructive. To understand how this might work, think of the Yellow River.

From time to time, the Yellow River would flood and devastate the lands around its banks, killing tens of thousands, but at other times, the same inexhaustible flow of water gives life to millions. Bad things happen, just as good things do – it is all part of nature. However, some remarkable individuals, such as Yu the Great, can use their skill and ingenuity to control a flood on a particular occasion and so not only save lives, but divert the waters into dikes and irrigation channels, thereby transforming a bad outcome into good. Such interventions are as natural as the flood itself and in fact they can only succeed if the man who intervenes is himself in tune with the Dao.

When the natural impulse for violence is redirected, it can serve other purposes, enabling us to compete with each other, challenge orthodoxy, come up with new ideas and create new things. All life is a kind of war. Business is war, politics is war, love is war. So every area in our lives can benefit from the energy of our violent, competitive, aggressive impulse if it is controlled and channelled correctly.

In times of peace, then, the Chinese see the value in kung fu as a way to bring discipline, confidence, drive and focus to the practitioner. This is all part of the cultivation that the practitioner needs to undergo to become a Perfected Man.

There are alternative ways to carry out such cultivation, and both Daoism and Buddhism over the past two millennia have produced hundreds of manuals that purport to show how to do just that, whether through meditation, qi gong, or secret potions, mystic amulets or scrolls of spells. However, when taught properly, kung fu has an advantage over all of these methods: it acknowledges that violence is a natural part of human nature, so when that nature is being cultivated, the method used needs to account for the violence, too. If not, the human being will always be incomplete and so will never reach the status of the Perfected Man.

Chapter 13

The Kung Fu Method

This chapter tries to look back over the ideas and practices explored in this book and distil them into a kung fu method that can be applied not only to martial arts, but to other arts and disciplines as well.

In considering the philosophical underpinnings of kung fu we begin to see that kung fu as a discipline has more far-reaching objectives than just training to better someone in a fight. It is a method – one among many other rival methods, as we have seen – of becoming a Perfected Man. That is to say, its objective is to make the practitioner reach their full potential as a human being, by exploring those qualities that make a human being and developing and cultivating each one as far as it will go.

The Daoist concept of the Perfected Man has at its heart the insight that a man or woman becomes a human being through the way they live, and not just by virtue of birth. We are all born as an unworked lump of clay; it is how we mould and shape ourselves thereafter that makes us into something worthwhile.

As the impulse to violence is undeniably one of the most atavistic and deep-seated human traits, the kung fu method of self-cultivation has this in-built advantage over many other methods in that it does not leave this aspect out. The Perfected Man cultivated via the kung fu method therefore is complete, whereas other methods, such as Za Zen meditation in pursuit of enlightenment or alchemy in pursuit of immortality, prefer to pretend that violence is not part of human nature, or, if they accept that it is, they prefer to think it has no benefits whatsoever and so should just be purged during the cultivation process. As a martial artist, I know different, aware as I am from personal experience in how many different ways the martial impulse can be fruitfully applied even in a time of peace.

The Six Areas of Cultivation in Kung Fu

So, as far as the kung fu method is concerned, what are the areas you try to cultivate to become a Perfected Man?

The **first area of cultivation**, as we have seen, is the internal cultivation, nei gong, of your heart/mind (xing), your body and your breath (qi). This is inward looking and private to you as an individual.

The **second area of cultivation** is expanding your inner cultivation to connect with the world around you, by finding your true place in the Pattern, and then living your life in tune with the Dao. From this comes naturalness and intuitiveness.

This is not enough, however, for as Lao Zi and Zhuang Zi both teach, it is not the true Daoist way to fully sequester yourself from the rest of human society (as we have seen, this is an area in which Daoism is often misunderstood). Rather you need to show compassion for your fellow man and work to help society, but in a very specific way: not by rules and regulations or the creation of ideologies that are forced down people's throats whether or not they fit the context, but by leading through De (in Lao Zi's terms) or changing things through your daemonic nature (in Zhuang Zi's terms), which also need to be cultivated. This is the **third area of cultivation**, and any teacher or leader needs to understand this lesson.

The **fourth area of cultivation** is filial piety and brotherhood, the social rules and obligations that tie you to your fellow students and to your master. These too need to be cultivated, because a Perfected Man does not become such in isolation, but with the assistance of others, and should in return provide such assistance to the next generation that follows.

The **fifth area of cultivation** is the adherence to patterns passed down by previous generations. While you are still engaged in the process of cultivation, the rules and rituals of your inherited patterns, combined with filial piety, give you the discipline and focus to stick to the correct path and achieve the desired transmission of knowledge from your master.

The **sixth area of cultivation,** as we discussed, is the one that is unique to the kung fu method: the taking control of and harnessing your natural impulse for violence. This is what gives you the courage, energy, drive, spirit and fire you need to succeed.

These six areas of cultivation make up the kung fu method of becoming a Perfected Man. Some martial artists would no doubt add others or rename and rephrase some of these areas to suit their personal experience. That is fine, but at the core, all of these six need to be present.

Many would argue that some of these six would seem to contradict others, but if we dig a little deeper, such seeming contradictions disappear.

We have already discussed how channelling violence, for example, does not contradict the principle of compassion but rather works with it. Likewise, in another apparent contradiction, the requirement to follow set patterns and rituals and so learn discipline does not, in fact, contradict the naturalness of following the Way, because the Way itself underpins the main Pattern of which all other lesser patterns are representations. As a martial artist, as we have seen, you need to learn discipline and internalise it before you are able to let it go and achieve freedom and intuitiveness. Similarly, there is no contradiction between filial piety and freedom, for, as we have shown, an individual chooses to submit and, by choosing to do so, his freedom is fully realised rather than being suppressed. In this way, all six principles work together and are self-reinforcing.

Applying the Kung Fu Method in Life

There is no set time for how long it takes you to become a Perfected Man; the only limit is set by the extent of your own lifetime. Nor is it something that you achieve and can then let go of and forget about, resting on the laurels of your "achievement." Rather it is a continuous process of self-perfection. As my master often says: "you train until you die."

Also it is important to understand that the kung fu method is not something you only do during martial arts training. The six principles described above need to pervade every aspect of your life: your friendships and relationships, your work, your study, your hobbies.

As we have already mentioned, you can still come across instances in China today when a master calligrapher, musician or a wood carver is said to have good kung fu. Does this mean that the kung fu method we have outlined can be pursued outside of martial arts, by applying yourself to one of these other skills or arts to reach the stage of a Perfected Man?

Lets consider the example of a calligrapher. You need to have studied different styles of calligraphy and copied out the work of previous great masters as part of your training – this is your cultivation of the pattern, internalising and making your own the requisite skills.

In studying your chosen art, you will have needed to follow a master, which entails practising filial piety.

You need to achieve the focus and calmness of mind and the full control of your own faculties – your body, mind and breath – that comes through internal cultivation.

You need to be in tune with the Way, making the movements of your brush natural and intuitive and give the quality of rightness to the strokes your brush leaves on the page.

You seek to influence people who see your finished work, to bring about the right emotional response – so you will need to apply your De and your compassion for and empathy with the feelings of others.

Finally, you will be competing with others in your art and need the drive and fire necessary to establish your name among many others.

As such, we can see that all six areas of cultivation we have identified can be applied to calligraphy just as readily as to martial arts.

This has long been recognised by Chinese masters of both arts. For example, the famous Tang Dynasty calligrapher Zhang Su (Chang Hsu) was said to have "found inspiration in the rhythmic movements of the sword dance, recognizing a kinship between the two arts as an expression of inner vitality."[1]

Similar examples can be given for many other Chinese traditional arts, such as music, poetry and weiqi.

The most famous example of the kung fu method outside a martial context is, however, nothing as refined as a calligrapher or a poet, but the humble aspect of a cook that Zhuang Zi uses to explain the state of being a Perfected Man.

So important I think this passage is to philosophy of kung fu and the kung fu method that it is worth quoting the story here in full before we consider its meaning:

"Cook Ting was carving an ox for Lord Wen-hui. As his hand slapped, shoulder lunged, foot stamped, knee crooked, with a hiss! With a thud! The brandished blade as it sliced never missed the rhythm, now in time with the Mulberry Forest dance, now with an orchestra playing the Ching-shou.

"'Oh, excellent!' said Lord Wen-hui. 'That skill should attain such heights!'

"'What your servant cares about is the Way, I have left skill behind me. When I first began to carve oxen, I saw nothing but oxen wherever I looked. Three years more and I never saw an ox as a whole. Nowadays, I am in touch through the daemonic in me, and do not look with the eye. With the senses I know where to stop, the daemonic I desire to run its course. I rely on Heaven's structuring, cleave along the main seams, let myself be guided by the main cavities, go by what is inherently so. A ligament or tendon I never touch, not to mention solid bone. A good cook changes his chopper once a year, because he hacks. A common cook changes it once a month, because he smashes. Now I have had this chopper for nineteen years, and have taken apart several thousand oxen, but the edge is as though it were fresh from the grindstone. At that joint there is an interval, and the chopper's edge has no thickness; if you insert what has no thickness where there is an interval, then, what more could you ask, of course there is ample room to move the edge about. That's why after nineteen years the edge of my chopper is as though it were fresh from the grindstone.

"'However, whenever I come to something intricate, I see where it will be hard to handle and cautiously prepare myself, my gaze settles on it, action slows down for it, you scarcely see the flick of the chopper – and at one stroke the tangle has been unravelled, as a clod crumbles to the ground. I stand chopper in hand, look proudly round at everyone, dawdle to enjoy the triumph until I'm quite satisfied, then clean the chopper and put it away.'

"'Excellent!' said Lord Wen-hui. 'Listening to the words of Cook Ting, I have learned from them how to nurture life.'"[2]

Many scholars, including Angus Graham himself, and both Puett and Eno whom we considered earlier, see this chapter as explaining one of the main tenets of Zhuang Zi's philosophy.

The art of butchery that Cook Ding possesses is an everyday skill, and Zhuang Zi very purposefully chooses it over more refined and exclusive skills, for example music or poetry, to illustrate the point he was making, namely, that the state of the Perfected Man, when you get in tune with the Dao, can be achieved by anyone at all, and that it requires not a noble birth or a secret teaching but years of dedication. It requires years of honing whatever given skill you start with, until you tune your mind, body and breath (qi) to your art to such a degree that you and your art become one, and it is at that moment of transcendence that you are temporarily in touch with the Dao.

For if the Dao is anything, it is change. By honing your skill – whatever it is, whether butchery or pottery or martial arts – you become a perfect agent of change, an agent of transformation, turning a meat carcass into a meal, clay into a pot, strings into music; and a fist or a sword into victory over your opponent and life for yourself, where before it hung in the balance. It is in a very real sense a kind of alchemy, where one thing is transformed into another.

It is interesting to note that time and gradual development of the skill play an important part in the story of Cook Ding. It is made very clear that he did not become this good straight away, but rather went through a gradual process of transformation over a number of years. Kirkland points out that this gradual transformation is a very Daoist approach and one area where Daoism contrasts with Chan or Zen Buddhism: for the latter, the gaining of enlightenment was achieved all at once in a sudden flash of inspiration, not in a lengthy process of trial and error, practice and self-perfection.[3]

At this point it is worth considering a counter-example to this method of self-cultivation through the practice of a skill. Lorge mentions a story from the Song Dynasty, of a young scholar called Chen Yaozi – a historical figure who was born in 970 – practising archery in his garden. Such was his skill that every arrow reached the perfect centre of the target. The scholar's practice was observed by a passing oil peddler, who then went on to criticise what he saw:

"When Chen asked whether he knew something about archery, the peddler discounted Chen's skill as merely the product of practice, Chen was incensed that the peddler scorned his accuracy. The peddler thereupon put a coin (Chinese coins had a square hole in the middle) over the opening of a gourd and ladled oil into it without touching the sides. This was easy, the peddler related, because he practiced this task all the time. Physical skills, in this perspective, might seem impressive, but in reality are quite banal."[4]

Lorge goes on to say that this story "is well known to all Taiwanese school children, and many in China as well. It makes a fundamental value judgement in favour of studying over physical pursuits."[5]

How then can this challenge be answered? What is different between Cook Ding's experience and that of the oil peddler?

The answer, I believe, lies in these two lines from the story of Cook Ding, from the full quote given above:

"'Oh, excellent!' said Lord Wen-hui. 'That skill should attain such heights!'
'What your servant cares about is the Way, I have left skill behind me [Cook Ding replies]...'"

Both the oil peddler and the cook through practice have improved their skill in their particular pursuit to such a level that other people were amazed to see it, but the peddler stopped there, while the cook took the next step and drew from his practice the "extrovertive" – to borrow Roth's terminology we last encountered in Chapter 3 in discussing the *Neiye* – mystical experience of unity with the Way. It is that step that makes the practice of a skill a means of self-cultivation.

Kirkland summarises this well:

"In Taoism, the fundamental activity in which one ideally engages is a *cultivation of reality*, which takes place through a newly experiential engagement with a specific set of subtle forces, structures, and energies, which are inherent to one's personal reality... In Taoism, *both* one's body (or, more properly, one's body/heart/mind/energy/spirit) *and* the social, political, and physical matrices within which one's personal life take [sic] place – i.e., realities that Taoists often called one's *ming*, "facts that cannot be changed" – are deemed not only to be real and important, but, in certain key ways, fundamental to one's practice of personal transformation."[6]

What does this all mean? It means that when becoming a Perfected Man you learn to experience reality differently from others. You not only no longer see your given position in life a limitation, but you actively make use of whatever you have as part of transforming yourself. Ding was a cook and not a Lord, but he made the most of his position, by perceiving the very state of being a cook and butchering meat as a pathway to enlightenment. The oil peddler, however, made no such experiential shift.

Limits of the Kung Fu Method

However, there are some limits. It is important to note that the kung fu method cannot be applied to a purely intellectual discipline such as, say, mathematics, because it requires the training of the body and not just the mind.

A key part of what you are training is the body's movement, whether as a fighter, choosing when and where to strike, or as a wood carver, choosing where and how deeply to apply your cutter to the wood, or as a musician, choosing which string to pluck.

As with the cultivation and the overcoming of the violent impulse, so the cultivation of the physical movement of the body is not part of all methods to become a Perfected Man, but physicality of movement is as fundamental to human nature as is violence, so again, the kung fu method, by including it and focusing on it no less than on mental and spiritual cultivation, can be seen to be a more holistic approach than other non physical methods for achieving the state of a Perfected Man such as static meditation or the alchemy of wai dan.

Another limitation in applying the kung fu method is that the skill, art or discipline we seek to apply it to has to be one that can be improved through effort and over time, rather than one you can achieve immediately and automatically.

Some human beings are lucky enough to be born with natural or genetic gifts and talents from perfect pitch to photographic memory. As long as such talents still need to be shaped and the individual concerned applies the effort, then the kung fu method can be used on such a skill or talent so that the individual can become through it a Perfected Man. If, however, the individual does not apply themselves and merely falls back on the natural skills given them by nature, then they cannot be said to be a Perfected Man.

One last limit is that the skill or art you are engaged in needs to be carried out within a society and needs to be valued by that society. Practising a skill in seclusion, unknown to others, is not the kung fu method, no matter how good you become.

Since you are not engaging with others, you cannot demonstrate true compassion, nor can you influence them through your De. Nor, finally, are you in competition with anyone, so your skill is not measured and tested against that of your peers.

Your community, after all, is part of Kirkland's aforementioned "social, political, and physical matrices" in which you live your life, and so is part of what you are cultivating.

We can summarise, then, that the kung fu method has the objective of becoming a Perfected Man by undertaking cultivation in six key areas, and this method can be used with any skill or art that requires the application of mind, body and spirit in a diligent and disciplined effort to attain perfection, so long as this art or skill is performed not in isolation but within the society of its day.

Having arrived at a definition of what the kung fu method is, it is important to understand that teaching the kung fu method does not mean abandoning kung fu as a martial art and turning it into just a philosophic pursuit. Although it is applicable through other skills and practices, it is as a martial art that it was originally conceived, and it is as a martial art that it is most potent.

The role of a human being as a fighter and as a hunter is one of the oldest that our ancestors have acted out. As such, the art of kung fu as a martial path is the "elder brother" of most if not all other arts (the only exception perhaps being the art of a shaman) and so the kung fu of poetry and of calligraphy, of carving and of music, of statesmanship and of strategy all owe allegiance to it.

Instead of displacing the martial aspect, the kung fu method applied in other spheres helps to balance it out, allowing us to harmonise everything we do in our lives, which in turn enriches our insight as martial artists.

Martial arts students always ask how often they should practise, how many hours a day, how many days a week, to become good.

The correct answer is every hour, every day. And this is not to say that we expect the students not to eat or sleep, but that they should adopt the kung fu method into every aspect of their lives. As the Daoist relates to the Way, so the martial artist relates to kung fu: there is no point at which you are not living it.

Conclusion

In tracing the history of kung fu and exploring some key ideas of its philosophy, I hope this book has been able to show the richness of its heritage and how connected it is to Chinese culture as a whole.

However, kung fu as a discipline that has lasted for so many generations is under threat in the modern world, with two arguments levelled against it (as against all martial arts).

One arises out of prejudice and misunderstanding, namely that kung fu is violent, thuggish and dangerous and has no place in a civilised society, particularly in our time of peace and plenty.

The second is that it is redundant as a martial discipline in a time of tanks, missiles, guns and fighter jets outside specific cases such as sport, or training for the army.

Such challenges undermine kung fu's standing and reputation among the wider population. This inevitably raises the question of whether this ancient art is doomed to irrelevance, following in the wake of so many traditional martial arts of other nations that came up against and lost the struggle with modernity.

The answer is that if kung fu is practised as no more than a skilful way of waving a sword or throwing a punch, then such irrelevance may well come one day.

As the older generations of masters pass, they will take many of their skills with them. That is not fatal in itself; skills are lost with every generation, but they are then rediscovered, reinvented and perhaps improved upon by those who come after.

However, that assumes that the environment requires them.

Masters now in their sixties, seventies and eighties were born into a harsher and less certain world, where physical violence was rife and kung fu was called into action again and again. Their environment required such skills and honed them through necessity; does ours?

For many of us, the answer is almost certainly not. This means that, as that generation passes, we who replace them will not be able to reinvent ourselves in the same way.

There will be residual memory for a while, but eventually the time will come when the comfort and the distractions of the modern lifestyle will take their toll.

But ironically, our comfortable and distracted life of computers, television and ready meals is exactly when we most need the discipline and the physicality of kung fu. Our children are in danger of growing up as blobs, existing but not fully living in the real world, and preferring the exciting but safe certainties and the absence of consequences of the virtual world of the internet.

And those are the "lucky" ones, with other children growing up no less disconnected with the real world of consequences, but without the parental support and material resources that make them safe, and instead roaming the streets of our inner cities as warriors without a war. Boys (and they are mostly, though not exclusively, boys) who are desperate to prove their masculinity in a world that does not give a damn about helping them find it in something constructive.

How much they could use the strictures of striving for self-betterment, of discipline, confidence and self-respect, of the code of brotherhood, compassion and filial piety, and the mastering of their natural violent impulses that kung fu can offer!

So, at the time of our greatest need of what it offers, kung fu is in danger of petering out, of losing its potency. The current generation of practitioners must not let it happen. The key to this is remembering that kung fu has never been just about throwing that punch, but, as this book has attempted to demonstrate, a culture unto itself and a way of living your life.

We may not be as good at sword fighting as our ancestors in the Warring States or the Three Kingdoms, because we no longer live by the sword, but we can and must reinvent kung fu in our own image and make it relevant again.

We will not be unique in having to do this. Every dynasty in the long history of China has had to do the same. The fighters of the Three Kingdoms would not have had the skills with the chariot that their Zhou and Shang ancestors possessed but excelled in horsemanship; the fighters of the Qing Dynasty did not have the artistry with the sword or the bow that the Tang Dynasty had, but they excelled in open-hand techniques.

In a period of relative peace, the key to the survival of kung fu is the knowledge of the kung fu method and the ability to suffuse your whole life with its practice and not just the hours we spend in the training hall or the competition arena. It may just be the way to let our young rediscover themselves and the amazing abilities their minds, bodies and spirits can give them in everything they do.

As was said before, this does not mean turning our back on kung fu as the art of fighting. The ability to fight will always be a crucial part of what is imparted and precisely the means through which latent violence is harnessed and channelled into something positive. And if we practise the kung fu method correctly, we will adhere to our patterns and have the filial piety to preserve and pass down our styles, so if ever times change, and the martial aspect will need to predominate again, it will be there and ready at the core of what we do.

In this way, kung fu assumes its true meaning as an art of living as well as an art of fighting.

The only way to achieve this, however, is for the rest of society to give up its prejudice that kung fu is somehow a thuggish sport. And the way to achieve that is to educate society about the cultural richness of kung fu and the benefits its philosophy can have for all of us, particularly for the younger generation.

To be convincing, practitioners themselves first need to reconnect with the full richness of kung fu culture and understand its history. This short book can never hope to capture all there is to know about kung fu, but if it serves as a trigger to make you as a reader think about exploring this culture further, then it will have served its purpose.

And, to my mind, there is no better place to start the exploration than the *Zhuang Zi* and the *Neiye*, which should be regarded as core reading for all students of kung fu or any other martial art. Whereas the poetry of the *Zhuang Zi* paints the vision of what the practitioner should be striving for in becoming a Perfected Man, the *Neiye* begins to map out the way to get there.

Neither of these books would be a substitute for practice and direct transmission from a master – as both Zhuang Zi and the unknown writers of the *Neiye* would both say, I believe – but ignorance of them should be inexcusable for any serious student of kung fu.

End Notes

Preface and Acknowledgements

[1] Quote from Rhees, *Personal Recollections*, Ch. 6, cited in http://en.wikiquote.org/wiki/Ludwig_Wittgenstein

Introduction

[1] Barnes, *China, Korea and Japan: The Rise of Civilization in East Asia*, pp 108–113.

[2] Peers, *Soldiers of the Dragon: Chinese Armies 1500 BC–AD 1840*, p 19.

[3] Lorge, *Chinese Martial Arts: From Antiquity to the Twenty-First Century*, pp 197–202.

[4] Lorge, *Chinese Martial Arts: From Antiquity to the Twenty-First Century*, pp 198–202.

[5] Lorge, *Chinese Martial Arts: From Antiquity to the Twenty-First Century*, p 6.

[6] Lorge, *Chinese Martial Arts: From Antiquity to the Twenty-First Century*, p 49.

Chapter 1

[1] Barnes, *China, Korea and Japan: The Rise of Civilization in East Asia*, p 92.

[2] Fairbank, *China: A New History*, p 35.

[3] Walters, *An Encyclopedia of Myth and Legend: Chinese Mythology*, p 67.

[4] Cooper, *Chinese Alchemy: The Taoist Quest for Immortality*, p 16.

[5] Roth, *Original Tao: Inward Training (Nei-yeh) and the Foundation of Taoist Mysticism*, pp 6–8.

[6] Fairbank, *China: A New History*, p 35.

[7] Walters, *An Encyclopedia of Myth and Legend: Chinese Mythology*, p 175.

[8] Walters, *An Encyclopedia of Myth and Legend: Chinese Mythology*, p 101; Wang, *100 Chinese Gods*, p 19.

[9] Baynes, *I Ching or Book of Changes*, pp liii–liv.

[10] Graham, *Disputers of the Tao: Philosophical Argument in Ancient China*, pp 216–217.

[11] Roth, *Original Tao: Inward Training (Nei-yeh) and the Foundation of Taoist Mysticism*, pp 198–201.

[12] Allan, Introduction to Waley, Arthur, trans., *Confucius: The Analects*, p xii.

[13] Ripinsky-Naxon, *The Nature of Shamanism*, and Stutley, *Shamanism: an Introduction*.

[14] Stutley, *Shamanism: an Introduction*, p 2.

[15] Stutley, *Shamanism: an Introduction*, pp 22–23.

[16] Puett, *To Become a God: Cosmology, Sacrifice, and Self-Divinization in Early China*, first two chapters; Roth, *Original Tao: Inward Training (Nei-yeh) and the Foundation of Taoist Mysticism*, pp 189–190.

[17] Graham, *Disputers of the Tao: Philosophical Argument in Ancient China*, pp 100, 104.

[18] Puett, *To Become a God: Cosmology, Sacrifice, and Self-Divinization in Early China*, first two chapters.

[19] Firstly, as we have seen from some of the quotations I have given, Zhou Dynasty classics such as the *Guoyu*, the *Neiye*, the *Zhuang Zi* and the *Chuci* do mention elements such as spirit journeys and spirit possession, which are usually considered to be shamanic practices. From the Zhou Dynasty onwards, such elements have been key parts of Chinese cultural discourse, as evidenced by the "fashion" for writings produced through the method of spirit possession and trance until as late as the Qing Dynasty.

Secondly, the ancestors of the Chinese were surrounded by neighbouring people to whom they were related, who were practising shamanism and practise it still, particularly among Siberian tribes. We can be sure that such practices date back more than 10,000 years, since the Native American tribes who crossed the Bering Strait to the American continent at around that time still practise forms of shamanism that anthropologists consider to be directly related to that practised by their distant cousins in Siberia. It seems incredible that the Han Chinese, surrounded by shamanic practice on all sides for thousands of years, would somehow uniquely not practise it.

Thirdly, although I agree with Keightley and Puett that the earlier Shang bronze and bone inscriptions do not provide direct evidence of shamanic practices, but rather deal with ancestor worship and divination, I would argue that lack of clear textual evidence in the Shang inscriptions does not qualify as definitive evidence because the Shang inscriptions had a very narrow objective as records of divinations and ritual sacrifices only, rather than capturing the broader cultural activity of the time. If Keightly and Puett are right that the sacrificial and divination specialists were not shamans themselves, then that does not demonstrate that shamanic practices were not happening in other parts of society at the same time.

In fact, it would make sense, with the emergence of centralised political authority during the Xia and Shang dynasties, that shamanism, with its ideas of individual powers granted to the shaman by the spirits, would be seen as a rival source of power by the Xia and Shang kings and would more likely exist on the periphery of society than in the capital city making state sacrifices on behalf of the kings.

Finally, and on a purely personal basis as a practitioner of kung fu and qi gong, to me it seems likely that some elements of kung fu practice, such as animal-based taulu and daoyin exercises, like those in Hua Tuo's *Wuqin Xi* of the 2nd century AD, had something to do with the rituals of possession by animal spirits that are still practised by shamans to this day.

20 Lorge, *Chinese Martial Arts: From Antiquity to the Twenty-First Century*, p 5.

21 Graff, *Medieval Chinese Warfare, 300–900*, pp 21.

22 Peers, *Soldiers of the Dragon: Chinese Armies 1500 BC–AD 1840*, pp 19–32.

23 Peers, *Soldiers of the Dragon: Chinese Armies 1500 BC–AD 1840*, p 29.

24 Graff, *Medieval Chinese Warfare, 300–900*, p 21.

25 Lorge, *Chinese Martial Arts: From Antiquity to the Twenty-First Century*, pp 46–47.

26 Canzonieri, *Han Wei Wushu Newsletter*, Issue #23, Article #10, The emergence of Chinese martial arts.

27 Lorge, *Chinese Martial Arts: From Antiquity to the Twenty-First Century*, p 38.

28 Lorge, *Chinese Martial Arts: From Antiquity to the Twenty-First Century*, pp 40–42.

29 Lorge, *Chinese Martial Arts: From Antiquity to the Twenty-First Century*, pp 25–26.

30 Lorge, *Chinese Martial Arts: From Antiquity to the Twenty-First Century*, pp 25–26.

31 Lorge, *Chinese Martial Arts: From Antiquity to the Twenty-First Century*, p 28.

Chapter 2

1 Graff, *Medieval Chinese Warfare, 300–900*, p 21; Lewis, *The Early Chinese Empires: Qin and Han*, chapter 2.

2 Peers, *Soldiers of the Dragon: Chinese Armies 1500 BC–AD 1840*, pp 36–37.

3 Lewis, *The Early Chinese Empires: Qin and Han*, chapter 1.

4 Peers, *Soldiers of the Dragon: Chinese Armies 1500 BC–AD 1840*, p 34.

5 Peers, *Soldiers of the Dragon: Chinese Armies 1500 BC–AD 1840*, p34–35.

6   Peers, *Soldiers of the Dragon: Chinese Armies 1500 BC–AD 1840*, p 36.

7   Roth, *Original Tao: Inward Training (Nei-yeh) and the Foundation of Taoist Mysticism*, p 160.

8   Graff, *Medieval Chinese Warfare, 300–900*, pp 21–22.

9   Lewis, *The Early Chinese Empires: Qin and Han*, Chapter 2.

10 Hawkes, *The Songs of the South: An Anthology of Ancient Chinese Poems by Qu Yuan and Other Poets*.

11 Lorge, *Chinese Martial Arts: From Antiquity to the Twenty-First Century*, pp 62–63.

Chapter 3

1   Graham, *Chuang-Tzu: the Inner Chapters*, p 84.

2   In China the mind is associated with the heart rather than the head and the term "xing" covers both heart and mind at the same time.

3   Graham, *Chuang-Tzu: the Inner Chapters*, p 48.

4   Lau, *Lao Tzu: Tao Te Ching*, p 14.

5   Lau *Lao Tzu: Tao Te Ching*, p 62.

6   Roth, *Original Tao: Inward Training (Nei-yeh) and the Foundation of Taoist Mysticism*, p 21.

7   Various passages in Roth, *Original Tao: Inward Training (Nei-yeh) and the Foundation of Taoist Mysticism*, trace parallels in doctrine between the *Neiye* and the *Huai Nan Zi*, e.g., p 165; also, on p 168 there is an explicit statement that there was exchange of ideas between the centres where the classics were written: the Qi Xia Academy and the court of the Prince of Huai Nan; parallels also mentioned in Kirkland, *Taoism: the Enduring Tradition*, p 84.

8   Roth, *Original Tao: Inward Training (Nei-yeh) and the Foundation of Taoist Mysticism*, p 66.

9   Roth, *Original Tao: Inward Training (Nei-yeh) and the Foundation of Taoist Mysticism*, p 76

10 Roth, *Original Tao: Inward Training (Nei-yeh) and the Foundation of Taoist Mysticism*, p 78.

11 Roth, *Original Tao: Inward Training (Nei-yeh) and the Foundation of Taoist Mysticism*, p 82.

12 Roth, *Original Tao: Inward Training (Nei-yeh) and the Foundation of Taoist Mysticism*, p 109.

13 Roth, *Original Tao: Inward Training (Nei-yeh) and the Foundation of Taoist Mysticism*, p 128.

14 Roth, *Original Tao: Inward Training (Nei-yeh) and the Foundation of Taoist Mysticism*, p 109.

15 Roth, *Original Tao: Inward Training (Nei-yeh) and the Foundation of Taoist Mysticism*, p 110.

16 Roth, *Original Tao: Inward Training (Nei-yeh) and the Foundation of Taoist Mysticism*, p 90.

17 Roth, *Original Tao: Inward Training (Nei-yeh) and the Foundation of Taoist Mysticism*, p 179.

18 Roth, *Original Tao: Inward Training (Nei-yeh) and the Foundation of Taoist Mysticism*, p 183.

19 Roth, *Original Tao: Inward Training (Nei-yeh) and the Foundation of Taoist Mysticism*, p 4.

20 Robinet, quoted in Roth, *Original Tao: Inward Training (Nei-yeh) and the Foundation of Taoist Mysticism*, pp 122–123.

21 *Zhuang Zi*, quoted in Roth, *Original Tao: Inward Training (Nei-yeh) and the Foundation of Taoist Mysticism*, p 170.

22 Roth, *Original Tao: Inward Training (Nei-yeh) and the Foundation of Taoist Mysticism*, p 170.

23 Roth, *Original Tao: Inward Training (Nei-yeh) and the Foundation of Taoist Mysticism*, pp 161–162.

24 Kirkland, *Taoism: the Enduring Tradition*, p 84.

Chapter 4

1 Nylan, *The Five "Confucian" Classics*.

2 Paludan, *Chronicle of the Chinese Emperors: The Reign-by-Reign Record of the Rulers of Imperial China*, p 56.

[3] Lewis, *The Early Chinese Empires: Qin and Han*, chapter 6.

[4] Lorge, *Chinese Martial Arts: From Antiquity to the Twenty-First Century*, p 68.

[5] Lorge, *Chinese Martial Arts: From Antiquity to the Twenty-First Century*, pp 68–69.

[6] Shahar, *The Shaolin Monastery: History, Religion, and the Chinese Martial Arts*, p 140.

[7] Lorge, *Chinese Martial Arts: From Antiquity to the Twenty-First Century*, p 42.

[8] Wong, *Lieh-tzu*, p 58.

[9] Wong, *Lieh-tzu*, p 3.

[10] Incorporation of internal cultivation theories into *Huai Nan Zi* mentioned in Puett, *To Become a God: Cosmology, Sacrifice, and Self-Divinization in Early China*, pp 260–284; and also in Le Blanc, *Huai Nan Tzu: Philosophical Synthesis in Early Han Thought*, p 8.

[11] *Huai Nan Zi*, "Qisu" chapter, 11.9b, quoted in Puett, *To Become a God: Cosmology, Sacrifice, and Self-Divinization in Early China*, p 218.

[12] *Huai Nan Zi*, quoted in Cleary, *Classics of Strategy and Counsel*, p 10.

[13] Puett, *To Become a God: Cosmology, Sacrifice, and Self-Divinization in Early China*.

[14] Lorge, *Chinese Martial Arts: From Antiquity to the Twenty-First Century*, pp 40–43.

[15] Shahar, *The Shaolin Monastery: History, Religion, and the Chinese Martial Arts*, p156.

[16] Shahar, *The Shaolin Monastery: History, Religion, and the Chinese Martial Arts*, p 156.

[17] Lorge, *Chinese Martial Arts: From Antiquity to the Twenty-First Century*, p 119.

[18] Lorge, *Chinese Martial Arts: From Antiquity to the Twenty-First Century*, p 178.

[19] Lorge, *Chinese Martial Arts: From Antiquity to the Twenty-First Century*, p 192.

Chapter 5

1 Besio and Tung, eds., *Three Kingdoms and Chinese Culture*, p xx.
2 Graff, *Medieval Chinese Warfare, 300–900*, p 17.
3 Graff, *Medieval Chinese Warfare, 300–900*, p 35.
4 Besio and Tung, eds., *Three Kingdoms and Chinese Culture*, p xviii.
5 Tillman, "Selected Historical Sources for *Three Kingdoms*: Reflections from Sima Guang's and Chen Liang's Reconstructions of Kongming's Story," in Besio and Tung, eds., *Three Kingdoms and Chinese Culture*, pp 53–67.
6 Kirkland, *Taoism: the Enduring Tradition*, pp 84–87.
7 *Bao Pu Zi*, ed. De Bary, *Sources of Chinese Tradition, Volume I*, p 261.
8 Shahar, *The Shaolin Monastery: History, Religion, and the Chinese Martial Arts*, pp 11–12.
9 Shahar, *The Shaolin Monastery: History, Religion, and the Chinese Martial Arts*, pp 162–163.
10 Shahar, *The Shaolin Monastery: History, Religion, and the Chinese Martial Arts*, p 149.
11 Shahar, *The Shaolin Monastery: History, Religion, and the Chinese Martial Arts*, pp 35–36.
12 Shahar, *The Shaolin Monastery: History, Religion, and the Chinese Martial Arts*, pp 36–37, translated from Chaoye qian zai, 2.21–22.
13 Shahar, *The Shaolin Monastery: History, Religion, and the Chinese Martial Arts*, p 37.

Chapter 6

1 Paludan, *Chronicle of the Chinese Emperors: The Reign-by-Reign Record of the Rulers of Imperial China*, pp 98–101.
2 Cooper, Arthur, trans., *Li Po and Tu Fu*.

3   Kirkland, *Taoism: the Enduring Tradition*, pp 95–96 and pp 153–158.
4   Shahar, *The Shaolin Monastery: History, Religion, and the Chinese Martial Arts*, p 22.
5   Grigg, *The Tao of Zen*.
6   Fahr-Becker, *The Art of East Asia*, section on Japanese Art.
7   Paludan, *Chronicle of the Chinese Emperors: The Reign-by-Reign Record of the Rulers of Imperial China*, p 108–109.
8   Shahar, *The Shaolin Monastery: History, Religion, and the Chinese Martial Arts*, p 19.
9   Shahar, *The Shaolin Monastery: History, Religion, and the Chinese Martial Arts*, pp 23–24.
10 Shahar, *The Shaolin Monastery: History, Religion, and the Chinese Martial Arts*, p 24.
11 Lorge, *Chinese Martial Arts: From Antiquity to the Twenty-First Century*, p 173.
12 Shahar, *The Shaolin Monastery: History, Religion, and the Chinese Martial Arts*, p 56.
13 Lorge, *Chinese Martial Arts: From Antiquity to the Twenty-First Century*, pp 173–174.
14 Lorge, *Chinese Martial Arts: From Antiquity to the Twenty-First Century*, p 132.
15 Lorge, *Chinese Martial Arts: From Antiquity to the Twenty-First Century*, p 103.
16 Lorge, *Chinese Martial Arts: From Antiquity to the Twenty-First Century*, pp 132–133.
17 Kirkland, *Taoism: the Enduring Tradition*, p 95.
18 Huang Zongxi, "Epitaph for Wang Zhengnan," tr. in Douglas Wile, *T'ai Chi's Ancestors*, New York: Sweet Ch'i Press, 1999, 53, quoted in Lorge, *Chinese Martial Arts: From Antiquity to the Twenty-First Century*, p 192.
19 Lorge, *Chinese Martial Arts: From Antiquity to the Twenty-First Century*, p 103.
20 Yumoto, *The Samurai Sword: A Handbook*, p 27.

21 Peers, *Soldiers of the Dragon: Chinese Armies 1500 BC–AD 1840*, pp 115–118.

22 Peers, *Soldiers of the Dragon: Chinese Armies 1500 BC–AD 1840*, p 115.

23 Peers, *Soldiers of the Dragon: Chinese Armies 1500 BC–AD 1840*, p 129.

24 Peers, *Soldiers of the Dragon: Chinese Armies 1500 BC–AD 1840*, p 130.

Chapter 7

1 Lewis, *The Early Chinese Empires: Qin and Han*, location 185.

2 Paludan, *Chronicle of the Chinese Emperors: The Reign-by-Reign Record of the Rulers of Imperial China*, p 138.

3 Menzies, *1421: The Year China Discovered the World*.

4 Paludan, *Chronicle of the Chinese Emperors: The Reign-by-Reign Record of the Rulers of Imperial China*, p 187.

5 Lorge, *Chinese Martial Arts: From Antiquity to the Twenty-First Century*, p 134.

6 The information on style histories in these few paragraphs is based on own research in Fujian and elsewhere in China for *Wushu Scholar Magazine*.

7 Yang Jwing-Ming, *Ancient Chinese Weapons: A Martial Artist's Guide*, p 15.

8 Yang Jwing Ming, *Ancient Chinese Weapons: A Martial Artist's Guide*, pp 22–23.

9 Peers, *Soldiers of the Dragon: Chinese Armies 1500 BC–AD 1840*, pp 181–185.

10 Lorge, *Chinese Martial Arts: From Antiquity to the Twenty-First Century*, pp 113–118.

11 Peers, *Soldiers of the Dragon: Chinese Armies 1500 BC–AD 1840*, pp 180–181.

12 Shahar, *The Shaolin Monastery: History, Religion, and the Chi-*

nese Martial Arts, pp 56–67, and Lorge, *Chinese Martial Arts: From Antiquity to the Twenty-First Century*, pp 167–182.

13 Shahar, *The Shaolin Monastery: History, Religion, and the Chinese Martial Arts*, p 55.

14 Shahar, *The Shaolin Monastery: History, Religion, and the Chinese Martial Arts*, pp 64–65.

15 Shahar, *The Shaolin Monastery: History, Religion, and the Chinese Martial Arts*, pp 65–66.

16 Shahar, *The Shaolin Monastery: History, Religion, and the Chinese Martial Arts*, pp 68–70.

17 Shahar, *The Shaolin Monastery: History, Religion, and the Chinese Martial Arts*, p 55.

18 Kirkland, *Taoism: the Enduring Tradition*, pp 98–113.

19 Paludan, *Chronicle of the Chinese Emperors: The Reign-by-Reign Record of the Rulers of Imperial China*, p 160.

Chapter 8

1 Paludan, *Chronicle of the Chinese Emperors: The Reign-by-Reign Record of the Rulers of Imperial China*, p 193.

2 Peers, *Soldiers of the Dragon: Chinese Armies 1500 BC–AD 1840*, p 235.

3 Paludan, *Chronicle of the Chinese Emperors: The Reign-by-Reign Record of the Rulers of Imperial China*, pp 191–197.

4 Paludan, *Chronicle of the Chinese Emperors: The Reign-by-Reign Record of the Rulers of Imperial China*, p 208.

5 Paludan, *Chronicle of the Chinese Emperors: The Reign-by-Reign Record of the Rulers of Imperial China*, p 215.

6 Paludan, *Chronicle of the Chinese Emperors: The Reign-by-Reign Record of the Rulers of Imperial China*, pp 210–216.

7 Own research conducted in Fujian and elsewhere in China for *Wushu Scholar Magazine*.

8 Shahar, *The Shaolin Monastery: History, Religion, and the Chinese Martial Arts*, p 184.

9 Own research conducted in Fujian and elsewhere in China for *Wushu Scholar Magazine.*

10 Shahar, *The Shaolin Monastery: History, Religion, and the Chinese Martial Arts*, pp 42–52, Lorge, *Chinese Martial Arts: From Antiquity to the Twenty-First Century*, pp 173–175 and 203.

1 Shahar, *The Shaolin Monastery: History, Religion, and the Chinese Martial Arts*, pp 234–235.

12 Kirkland, *Taoism: the Enduring Tradition*, pp 114–115.

13 Kirkland, *Taoism: the Enduring Tradition*, p 113.

14 Shahar, *The Shaolin Monastery: History, Religion, and the Chinese Martial Arts*, p 148.

15 Shahar, *The Shaolin Monastery: History, Religion, and the Chinese Martial Arts*, p 149.

16 Shahar, *The Shaolin Monastery: History, Religion, and the Chinese Martial Arts*, p 153.

17 This is based on own research in Fujian Province for *Wushu Scholar Magazine*, but Patrick McCarthy presents the same information in the introduction to *The Bible of Karate: Bubishi*, pp 34–35.

18 Bishop, *Okinawan Karate: Teachers, styles and secret techniques*, pp 19–43.

19 McCarthy, *The Bible of Karate: Bubishi*, pp 24–42.

Chapter 9

1 Graham, *Disputers of the Tao*, pp 319–325.

2 Freedman, *On the sociological study of Chinese religion*, pp 34–40.

3 Kirkland, *Taoism: the Enduring Tradition*, Introduction and Chapter 1.

4 Lau, *Lao Tzu: Tao Te Ching*, p 5.

5 Wittgenstein, *Tractatus Logico-Philosophicus* (1922) preface, quote taken from The Oxford Dictionary of Quotations.

6 Lau, *Lao Tzu: Tao Te Ching*, p 5.

[7] Wittgenstein, *Tractatus Logico-Philosophicus* (1922) p 148, quote taken from The Oxford Dictionary of Quotations.

[8] Cooper, *Chinese Alchemy: The Taoist Quest for Immortality*, pp 89–96.

[9] *Huai Nan Zi*, quoted in Major, *Heaven and Earth in Early Han Thought: Chapter Three, Four, and Five of the Huainanzi*, p 186–187.

Chapter 10

[1] Graham, *Chuang-Tzu: the Inner Chapters*, p 85.

[2] Graham, *Chuang-Tzu: the Inner Chapters*, p 85.

[3] Graham, *Chuang-Tzu: the Inner Chapters*, p 85.

[4] Graham, *Chuang-Tzu: the Inner Chapters*, p 58.

[5] Graham, *Chuang-Tzu: the Inner Chapters*, p 44.

[6] Puett, *To Become a God: Cosmology, Sacrifice, and Self-Divinization in Early China*, p 132.

[7] Graham, *Chuang-Tzu: the Inner Chapters*, p 53.

[8] Graham, *Chuang-Tzu: the Inner Chapters*, p 60.

[9] Lau, *Lao Tzu: Tao Te Ching*, p 64.

[10] Lau, *Lao Tzu: Tao Te Ching*, p 37.

[11] Graham, *Chuang-Tzu: the Inner Chapters*, p 46.

[12] Lau, *Lao Tzu: Tao Te Ching*, p 46.

[13] Lau, *Lao Tzu: Tao Te Ching*, p 15.

[14] Lau, *Lao Tzu: Tao Te Ching*, p 10.

[15] Lau, *Lao Tzu: Tao Te Ching*, p 12.

[16] Lau, *Lao Tzu: Tao Te Ching*, p 47.

Chapter 11

[1] Arthur Waley, *The Analects*, p 75.

[2] Allan, Introduction to Waley, Arthur, trans., *Confucius: The Analects,* p xix.

[3] Moss Roberts, "The Language of Values in the Ming Novel *Three*

Kingdoms" in Besio and Tung, eds., *Three Kingdoms and Chinese Culture*, p vii.

4 Moss Roberts, "The Language of Values in the Ming Novel *Three Kingdoms"* in Besio and Tung, eds., *Three Kingdoms and Chinese Culture*, pp vii–xiv.

5 Kirkland, *Taoism: the Enduring Tradition*, p 49.

6 Roth, *Original Tao: Inward Training (Nei-yeh) and the Foundation of Taoist Mysticism*, p 33.

7 *Xun Zi*, quoted in Roth, *Original Tao: Inward Training (Nei-yeh) and the Foundation of Taoist Mysticism*, p 33.

8 Roth, *Original Tao: Inward Training (Nei-yeh) and the Foundation of Taoist Mysticism*, p 30–31.

9 Graham, *Chuang-Tzu: the Inner Chapters*, p 70.

10 Graham, *Chuang-Tzu: the Inner Chapters*, p 71.

Chapter 12

1 Zhuge Liang, quoted in *Classics of Strategy and Counsel*, tr. Cleary, p 230.

2 Sun Wu, quoted in *Classics of Strategy and Counsel*, tr. Cleary, p 413.

3 Lin Wusun, *Sun Zi: The Art of War, Sun Bin: The Art of War: Two Chinese Military Classics in One Volume*, p 145–146.

4 Lau, *Lao Tzu: Tao Te Ching*, p 74.

5 Lau, *Lao Tzu: Tao Te Ching*, p 36.

6 Lau, *Lao Tzu: Tao Te Ching*, p 35.

7 Puett, *To Become a God: Cosmology, Sacrifice, and Self-Divinization in Early China*, p 133.

Chapter 13

1 Smith & Weng, *China: A History in Art*, p 140.

2 Graham, *Chuang-Tzu: the Inner Chapters*, pp 63–64.

3 Kirkland, *Taoism: the Enduring Tradition*, p 191.

4   Lorge, *Chinese Martial Arts: From Antiquity to the Twenty-First Century*, p 125.

5   Lorge, *Chinese Martial Arts: From Antiquity to the Twenty-First Century*, pp 125–126.

6   Kirkland, *Taoism: the Enduring Tradition*, p 194.

Index

124-127, 138, 147, 156, 163, 164, 168, 170, 172, 177; Daoist, 8, 10, 13, 24, 31, 38, 40, 43-45, 48-52, 54, 57, 59-61, 63, 74, 77, 79, 80, 82, 85, 91, 92, 106, 117, 125, 126, 134, 135, 138, 140, 143, 145, 155, 157, 158, 162-168, 171, 172, 177, 181; Daoists, 19, 24, 37, 39, 44, 49, 50-52, 72-74, 76, 78, 84, 116, 125, 127, 134, 136, 138, 153, 157, 164, 166, 168, 169; Daoist Sage, 23, 134; Daoist immortal, 69, 74, 125; Daojia vs Daojiao, 52; Dao Shu, 49, 52. *See also* Dao, Daoyin

Daoyin (= Daoist Gymnastics), 43, 57, 63, 64, 77, 79, 118, 189n.19; using Animal Forms, 57, 75, 189n.19. *See also* Hua Tuo, Wuqin Xi

De, 141, 142, 164, 165, 172, 174, 180

Dragon Style, 101

Eight Trigrams (*see* Ba Gua)

Ethics, 126, 147, 166-169; ethical, 160, 169. *See also* Compassion

Examinations: Civil Service, 54, 103; Military, 91, 93

Fang Qi Niang, 101

Filial Piety, 125, 126, 132, 147, 149-155, 158, 159, 168, 172-174, 184, 185; filial duty, 97; filial conduct, 158

Five Classics, 54, 156

Five Elements, 57, 119, 123, 124, 128-131, 145, 162; five phases, 130

Ge (= Dagger Axe), 9, 28

Ge Hong, 73-77, 80

Guan Dao, 72

Guan Yu, 70, 72, 153, 154

Guodian, 126

Han Fei Zi, 36

Huai Nan Zi (Book of), 13, 45,

49, 53, 60-65, 71, 72, 77-80, 130, 163, 191n.7, 193n.10

Health, 7, 11, 40, 46, 49, 51, 52, 77, 114. *See also* Longevity, Hygiene Practices, Daoyin

Huang Baijia, 106, 118

Huang Zhongxi, 63, 91, 106

Hua Tuo, 73-75, 80. *See also* Wuqin Xi, Daoyin

Huang Di (= Yellow Emperor), 19, 23, 54

Hung Gar, 113, 114

Hygiene practices, 49, 51, 74, 75, 163. *See also* Longevity, Health, Daoyin

Immortality, 57, 76, 137-140, 154, 172; immortal(s) 8, 19, 61, 69, 74, 75, 91, 125. *See also* Longevity, Health, Alchemy

Internal cultivation (*see* Nei gong)

Japan, 19, 84-86, 92, 93, 105, 119, 120, 126, 135

Jian (= straight sword), 3, 6, 29, 30, 40, 56, 62, 63, 84, 90, 92, 104, 161, 164, 175, 177, 183-185

Karate, xiii, 8, 102, 119, 120

Katana Sword, 92, 93

Koxinga (= General Zheng Chenggong), 109, 110

Lao Zi, 23-25, 38, 40, 43-45, 52, 125, 134, 140-142, 145, 158; and Huang Di, 19, 54; as Lao Tan, 24; and Tang Dynasty lineage, 84; and ethics/compassion, 164-166, 172; and warfare, 165

Lau Gar, 113

Lie Zi, 57, 59, 138

Lie Zi (Book of), 57, 62, 64, 65, 138

Li Bai, 84, 135

Li Shimin (*see* Tang Taizong)

Liu An (= King of Huai Nan), 45, 60, 61, 191n.7

Liu Bei, 69-72, 153, 154
Liu He Quan, 102
Longevity, 7, 13, 40, 50-52, 57, 75, 77. *See also* Daoyin, Immortality, Peng Zu
Lord Shang, 36
Manchu(s), 14, 95, 101, 107-109, 111, 112, 114, 117, 155
Martial Competitions, 31, 56, 91, 93; Hundred Events, 56; Entertainment Quarter demonstrations, 90, 91
Mawangdui, 64, 126
Meditation, 6, 8, 19, 26, 44, 48, 51, 52, 57, 65, 74, 79, 80, 106, 136, 170, 179; Za Zen, 85, 171
Mei Hua Quan, 114
Mencius, 31, 37, 38, 125, 156
Meng Zi (*see* Mencius)
Meng Zi (Book of), 13, 31, 62, 156
Military Strategy, 34, 40, 41, 56, 61, 63, 71, 72, 161-163, 181
Ming He Quan, 119. *See also* Crane Style
Monkey Style, 101
Nan Quan (= Southern Fist), 101; as southern styles, 75, 114
Nei gong (= Internal cultivation), xi, 6-13, 17, 25-27, 31-34, 39-41, 43-45, 47, 52, 53, 56, 57, 59, 60, 62-65, 71-75, 77-80, 82, 85, 91, 105, 106, 116-118, 120, 134, 137, 145, 147, 156, 157, 163, 172, 174. *See also* Perfected Man, Qi, Qi Gong, Daoyin, Nei Dan, *Neiye*
Nei dan (= Internal Alchemy), 52, 57, 74, 76, 77, 91, 116, 117, 138
Neiye, 13, 26, 27, 40, 43, 45-49, 51, 52, 57, 59, 61, 63, 71, 74, 75, 77, 80, 145, 156, 157, 178, 186, 188n.19, 191n.7
Open-hand fighting, 29, 79, 185;

wrestling, 8, 29, 56, 79, 86, 90; boxing (shoubo), 29, 56, 90, 92, 93, 102
Pattern (= subjective reality of perceptions and language), 124, 125, 127-129, 131, 132, 134, 151, 162, 172, 173
Pattern (= set movements in kung fu and other art forms) (*see* Taulu)
Peng Zu, 40, 57, 74, 163. *See also* Longevity, Hygiene Practices, Daoyin
Perfected Man (= Shen Ren), 44, 45, 127, 131, 134, 136-143, 145, 146, 153, 155, 158, 159, 162, 165, 166, 169-176, 179, 180, 186; self-perfection, 6, 31, 106, 135, 136, 141, 174, 177; perfection of skill, 41, 180; self-cultivation, 11, 31, 40, 45, 57, 62, 77, 142, 162, 163, 171, 177, 178. *See also* Nei gong
Pigua Quan, 5, 102
Qi, 5-9, 12, 13, 32, 48, 52, 60-63, 75, 78, 85, 118, 120, 124-126, 130, 156, 162, 172, 176
Qi gong, 43, 44, 48, 75-77, 106, 112, 118, 170, 189n19
Qi Jiguang, 63, 103
Qin Shi Huang Di, 19, 36-39
Sengchou, 79. *See also* Shaolin
Shamanism, 17, 25-27, 189n.19; shamanic, 13, 25-27, 31, 32, 39, 61, 75, 77, 125, 129, 188n.19, 189n.19; shaman, 25, 26, 51, 75, 129, 181, 189n.19; shamaness, 26. *See also* Dance
Shaolin: Monastery, 10, 78-80, 82, 84, 85, 88, 89, 91, 104, 105, 115, 116, 126; fighting monks, 56, 78-80, 88, 104, 105; kung fu (Shaolin Quan), 5, 78-80, 85, 89-91, 104, 105, 113, 126; staff, 104, 105; and internal cultivation, 79-81

Bibliography

Barnes, Gina L., *China, Korea and Japan: The Rise of Civilization in East Asia*, London: Thames and Hudson Ltd., 1993.

Baynes, trans., Wilhelm, Richard, *I Ching or Book of Changes*, Arkana, Penguin Group, 1989.

Besio, Kimberly Ann and Tung, Constantine, eds., *Three Kingdoms and Chinese Culture* [eBook edition], New York: State University of New York Press, 2007.

Bishop, Mark, *Okinawan Karate: Teachers, styles and secret techniques*, Second Edition. London: A & C Black, 1999.

Canzonieri, Salvatore. *The emergence of Chinese martial arts,* published in *Han Wei Wushu Newsletter*, Issue #23, Article #10, taken from the following link 22/03/2012: http://www.bgtent.com/natural-cma/CMAarticle10.htm

Cleary, Thomas, *Classics of Strategy and Counsel, Vol. 1*, Boston: Shambhala Publications, Inc., 2000.

Cooper, Arthur, trans., *Li Po and Tu Fu*, London: Penguin Books, 1973.

Cooper, J.C., *Chinese Alchemy: The Taoist Quest for Immortality*, Great Britain: Aquarian Press, part of the Thorsons Publishing Group, 1984.

De Bary, W.M. Theodore, ed., *Sources of Chinese Tradition, Volume I*, New York: Columbia University Press, 1960.

Fahr-Becker, Gabriele, ed., *The Art of East Asia*, Cologne: Koneman, 1999.

Fairbank, John K., *China: A New History*, Cambridge: Harvard University Press, 1992.

Freedman, Maurice, *On the sociological study of Chinese religion*, in Arthur P. Wolf, ed., *Religion and Ritual in Chinese Society*, Stanford: Stanford University Press, 1974.

Graff, David A., *Medieval Chinese Warfare, 300–900*, 1st ed., London and New York: Routledge, 2002 [eBook edition], Taylor & Francis e-Library, 2004.

Graham, A. C., *Disputers of the Tao: Philosophical Argument in Ancient China*, Chicago and La Salle, Illinois: Open Court Press, 1989.

Graham, A. C., trans. *Chuang-Tzu: the Inner Chapters*, Indianapolis/ Cambridge: Hackett Publishing Company, Inc., 2001.

Grigg, Ray, *The Tao of Zen*, This ed., Edison, NJ: Alva Press, 1999.

Hawkes, David, trans., *The Songs of the South: An Anthology of Ancient Chinese Poems by Qu Yuan and Other Poets*, Harmondsworth, England: Penguin Books Ltd., 1985.

Kirkland, Russell, *Taoism: The Enduring Tradition*, London and New York: Routledge, 2004.

Lau, D. C., trans., *Lao Tzu: Tao Te Ching*, London: Penguin Books, 1963.

Le Blanc, Charles, *Huai Nan Tzu: Philosophical Synthesis in Early Han Thought*, Hong Kong: Hong Kong University Press, 1985.

Lewis, Mark Edward, *The Early Chinese Empires: Qin and Han* [eBook edition], Cambridge, Massachusetts and London, England: The Belknap Press of Harvard University Press, 2007.

Lewis, Peter, *Myths and Legends of the Martial Arts*, London: Prion Books Limited, 1998.

Lin Wusun, trans. *Sun Zi: The Art of War, Sun Bin: The Art of War: Two Chinese Military Classics in One Volume*, Beijing: People's China Publishing House, 1995.

Lorge, Peter, *Chinese Martial Arts: From Antiquity to the Twenty-First Century*, Cambridge, New York: Cambridge University Press, 2012.

Major, John S., *Heaven and Earth in Early Han Thought: Chapter Three, Four, and Five of the Huainanzi*, Albany: State University of New York Press, 1993.

McCarthy, Patrick, *The Bible of Karate: Bubishi*, Boston; Rutland, Vermont; Tokyo: Tuttle Publishing, 1995.

Menzies, Gavin, *1421: The Year China Discovered the World*, Bantam Press, a division of Transworld Publishers, 2002.

Nylan, Michael, *The Five "Confucian" Classics*, New Haven & London: Yale University Press, 2001.

Paludan, Ann, *Chronicle of the Chinese Emperors: The Reign-by-Reign Record of the Rulers of Imperial China*, London: Thames & Hudson Ltd., 1998.

Partington, Angela, ed., *The Oxford Dictionary of Quotations*, revised fourth edition, Oxford University Press, 1996.

Peers, C.J., *Soldiers of the Dragon: Chinese Armies 1500 BC–AD 1840*. Oxford: Osprey Publishing, 2006.

Puett, Michael J., *To Become a God: Cosmology, Sacrifice, and Self-Divinization in Early China*, Harvard-Yenching Institute Monographs Series 57, Harvard University Press, 2002.

Rapinsky-Naxon, Michael, *The Nature of Shamanism: Substance and Function of a Religious Metaphor*, Albany: State University of New York Press, 1993.

Rhees, Rush, *Personal Recollections*, Ch. 6, 1981, cited in http://en.wikiquote.org/wiki/Ludwig_Wittgenstein

Roberts, Moss, "The Language of Values in the Ming Novel *Three Kingdoms*" in Besio, Kimberly Ann and Tung, Constantine, eds., *Three Kingdoms and Chinese Culture* [eBook edition], New York: State University of New York Press, 2007.

Roth, Harold D., *Original Tao: Inward Training (Nei-yeh) and the Foundation of Taoist Mysticism*, New York: Columbia University Press, 1999.

Shahar, Meir, *The Shaolin Monastery: History, Religion, and the Chinese Martial Arts*, Honolulu: University of Hawai'i Press, 2008.

Smith, Bradley and Weng, Wan-go, *China: A History in Art*, Gemini Smith Inc. and Wango Weng, 1979.

Stutley, Margaret., *Shamanism: An Introduction*, London and New York: Routledge, 2003.

Tillman, Hoyt Cleveland, "Selected Historical Sources for *Three Kingdoms*: Reflections from Sima Guang's and Chen Liang's Reconstructions of Kongming's Story," in Besio, Kimberly Ann and Tung, Constantine, eds., *Three Kingdoms and Chinese Culture* [eBook edition], New York: State University of New York Press, 2007.

Waley, Arthur, trans., Allan, Sarah, intr., *Confucius: The Analects*, 1st ed., George Allen & Unwin Ltd., 1938. Included in Everyman's Library, 2000.

Walters, Derek, *An Encyclopedia of Myth and Legend: Chinese Mythology*, 2nd ed., London: Diamond Books, 1995.

Wang, Xuewen and Wang, Yanxi, translators, Wu, Luxing, *100 Chinese Gods*, Singapore: Asiapac Books, 1994.

Wong, Eva, trans., *Lieh-tzu*, Boston & London: Shambhala Publications, 1995.

Wusun, Lin, trans., *Sun Zi: The Art of War, Sun Bin: The Art of War: Two Great Chinese Military Classics in One Volume*, Beijing: People's China Publishing House, 1995.

Yang, Jwing-Ming, *Ancient Chinese Weapons: A Martial Artist's Guide*, Boston: YMAA Publication Center, 1999.

Yumoto, John M., *The Samurai Sword: A Handbook*, Rutland, Vermont & Tokyo, Japan: Charles E. Tuttle Company, this ed. 1999.